Why Didn't I Just Raise Radishes

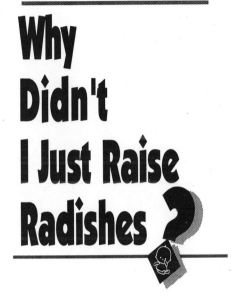

U NLESS WE CAN TOUCH and feel God in the commonplaces, he is going to be a very infrequent and unfamiliar guest. For life is made up of very ordinary experiences. Now and again a novelty leaps into the way, but the customary tenor is seldom broken. The ordinary stars shine upon us night after night; only occasionally does a comet come our way. Look at some of the daily commonplaces: health, sleep, bread and butter, work, friendship, a few flowers by the wayside, the laughter of children, the ministry of song, the bright day, the cool night. If I do not perceive God in these things, I have a very unhallowed and insignificant world.

—*John Henry Jowett*

Melodie M. Davis

Why Didn't I Just Raise Radishes?

Finding God in the Everyday

HERALD PRESS
Scottdale, Pennsylvania
Waterloo, Ontario

Library of Congress Cataloging-in-Publication Data
Davis, Melodie M., 1951-
    Why didn't I just raise radishes? / Melodie M. Davis.
        p. cm.
    ISBN 0-8361-3659-4 (alk. paper)
    1. Christian life—Meditations. 2. Motherhood—Religious
    aspects—Christianity—Meditations. I. Title.
BV4501.2.D385 1994
242—dc20   93-31064
                                                            CIP

The paper used in this publication is recycled and meets the
minimum requirements of American National Standard for Information Sciences—Permanence of Paper for Printed Library Materials,
ANSI Z39.48-1984.

WHY DIDN'T I JUST RAISE RADISHES?
Copyright © 1994 by Herald Press, Scottdale, Pa. 15683
        Published simultaneously in Canada by Herald Press,
        Waterloo, Ontario. N2L 6H7. All rights reserved
Library of Congress Catalog Number: 93-31064
International Standard Book Number: 0-8361-3659-4
Printed in the United States of America
Cover and book design by Paula M. Johnson

1 2 3 4 5 6 7 8 9 10 00 99 98 97 96 95 94

*To the girls
I wouldn't trade
for a bushel of radishes made of gold . . .
Michelle, Tanya, and Doreen.*

Contents

Preface

C OLUMNISTS ARE FREQUENTLY asked by readers if their columns will ever appear in a book. I know I find it difficult to remember to clip a piece that has inspired me. And I dare not do it immediately, because who likes to read a paper with holes all over it?

The one thing I don't like about writing a newspaper column is knowing my writing will soon line the bird cage or the cat box, or kindle a fire. Hence, this book, with columns turned into short meditations. I hope the book will help you look at ordinary daily events in new ways and thereby walk close to God.

One of my favorite columnists, theologian Martin E. Marty, detailed in a column all of the daily mundane chores he goes through in the process of getting up and going to work. He said, "Sure, a day in Cape Town, or Beijing or attending a presidential inauguration or a Super Bowl would be a highlight. But, overall, give most of us routine most of the time . . . pay attention to 'the ordinary' *as the arena of divine presence"* (emphasis added). That is what I hope this book will help us do—discover afresh God in our daily walk.

Thanks goes to daily companions at work and home who encouraged me as I sought a publisher for this project—Marian Bauman, typist for the book and administrative assistant; Paul Yoder and Lowell Hertzler who urged me to go for it; my boss, Ken Weaver; former co-worker Ron Byler, loyal promoter of my column; former co-worker, radio speaker, and columnist Margaret Foth, who turned the column opportunity over to me in 1987; helpful editor Michael A. King; and faithful readers who "consume" my meanderings.

Thanks also to my daughters, Michelle, Tanya, and Doreen, for inspiring me countless times in all the everyday events of our lives; to friends from whom I pick up snatches of conversation without always offering overt credit; and to my husband, Stuart, a solid rock I lean on, for allowing parts of our life to be made public.

—Melodie M. Davis
Harrisonburg, Virginia

Introduction

T HIS IS A BOOK GROUNDED in the everyday events of our
lives—a daughter having to wear flowered tennis
shoes to a fancy banquet, scrubbing the toilet bowl at
church, watching a spider catch flies in a web. Through
these everyday, even lowly, tasks and experiences we can
see God—if we're looking.

Most of life is made up of very ordinary days. Getting
up. Eating a quiet or hectic breakfast, depending on your
stage of life. Going to school or work. Having dinner. Re-
laxing or doing more work until bedtime.

A few of our days are spectacular: birth, wedding, becoming a Christian or confirming faith in Christ, first job,
retirement, death. These may be the *only* days that get
mentioned in the newspaper.

Most of us will never be famous. We will never live the
exciting and scandalous lives that we read about and
watch with alternating disgust and fascination.

How do we find God in the daily fabric of our lives?
An oracle in ancient times was a person through whom a
deity was believed to speak. In this book, the everyday

things that happen to us can be oracles, or messengers of God. Every day there are events that can be messengers of truth revealing motives, values, relationships, love, and faith.

Seeing God in everyday happenings begins by doing the obvious: talking to God, listening to God, reading the Bible. Finding God in nature is a favorite method of many, but millions live far removed from woods, creeks, and hills. So we also need to learn how to find God amidst concrete and asphalt. We need to recognize God's presence in the boardroom and the factory, in inner city schools and evening newscasts.

Many people who read my column say, "You write about such ordinary happenings," as if they are surprised anything special can come out of very ordinary days. This book is dedicated to helping you soak up more from all that is around you.

Made up of short readings, the pieces can be absorbed at whatever interval suits. Ideally you should allow enough time between them—perhaps a day—for reflection on the "oracles" that may be speaking to you.

I hope this book will enable you to see your daily events and circumstances in fresh ways. I hope you'll surprise yourself as you move to deeper levels of knowing God and closer to Thornton Wilder's "saints and poets who maybe do a better job of *realizing*" the joy and beauty of every minute as we live it. God is here.

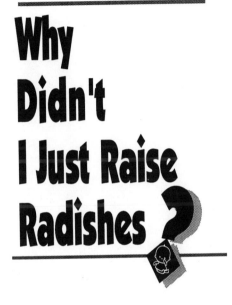

First Banquet, in Tennis Shoes

M Y EIGHT-AND-A-HALF-year-old daughter had accompanied me to a fancy hotel for a grown-up banquet. I thought she was ready for the experience of dining with three spoons and two forks, for not complaining about food set before her, and for listening to a Pulitzer Prize-winning journalist talk about the changing role of women in the media.

It was one of those "firsts" a parent treasures for a long time.

But it was *me*, not her, who almost made a big mistake.

Packing her suitcase without consulting her, I had thrown in a pair of dress shoes I thought still fit. As we hurried to get dressed at the hotel, she exclaimed, without tears, "Mama, these shoes don't fit me any more."

"Oh, really?" I said, panic level rising. "I thought you still wore them to church."

"No, Mama," she said like a teacher talking patiently to a student. "I wear the pink ones now."

So she did, I remembered too late.

"Well, you'll have to try to squeeze into these tonight," I ordered. "You aren't going to that banquet in flowered tennis shoes!"

To make more room, I told her to forget about socks. I felt like Cinderella's stepmother pushing my daughter's foot into that impossibly tight shoe.

She stood and limped to the bathroom. Ouch. I could tell she was upset, but she wasn't going to cry or pout and ruin her chance of going to this banquet.

Visions of the ancient practice of Chinese foot-binding of young girls filled my mind. Were we moderns any better off if we couldn't tolerate for one night an eight-year-old in comfortable tennis shoes at a black-tie banquet? What about the words of Jesus, "Why worry about clothes?"

"Oh well," I recanted in a sudden rush of empathy. "Just wear your tennis shoes." Her look of relief bound us together as sisters instead of mother and daughter. The mundane had been transformed to the magical.

I caught only one downward glance at the shoes in introducing my daughter to a group of media women. "Kids have a way of growing so fast," I explained, too quickly. "I didn't realize the shoes I brought for her were way too small!"

Several of the women shuffled their own feet squeezed into fancy dress shoes. "I wish *my* feet were in tennis shoes," one said sympathetically.

The rest of the evening was wonderful. Together Michelle and I admired the lovely banquet room and the place settings as I explained what each piece was for. Bravely she tasted the peanut soup, salad, country ham, and green beans. Brightly she conversed, answered questions, and tried to keep from interrupting me as well.

As symbolized by the too-tight shoes, children grow up almost without us being aware of it. Like Tevye in *Fiddler on the Roof* we ask, "I don't remember growing older —when did they?" Soon enough my daughter won't want to be caught at any banquet with her mother. So for now I'll savor the delight of watching my kid add her own special glow at the candlelit table, sneakers safely out of sight!

Does God ever marvel at my growth spurts? Do I embarrass the Almighty with my plodding and backsliding? Or maybe God understands these things better than any earthly parent and urges us on. We can celebrate this: just as we normally delight in and love our children, God delights in us even more.

VERSE FOR REFLECTION

The Lord delights in you and
will claim you as his own.
Isaiah 62:4 TLB

The "Hurry" in Us

WHEN OUR OLDEST daughter started going to school, we struggled constantly with morning routine. She got ready in slow motion; I operated on fast-forward. Finally in exasperation I observed, "What's wrong here is that all the *hurry* is in *me*. Don't you *realize* what will happen if you're late for school?"

So it was a great relief when daughter number two, after only a few weeks of kindergarten, started watching the clock in the morning with all the worry of a fast-track executive. "Come on," she'd tell her sister ten minutes before the bus was due. "The big hand is straight up and the bus is coming!" With that she'd hurry out the door.

Genetic differences? Environmental changes? Why did daughter two have more hurry in her? Thank goodness for small miracles.

Then daughter number three made me look at things another way. I was taking her to the doctor one day when

I was on an even tighter schedule than most days. I knew if I was late for the first appointment, the rest of the day would be thrown off, perhaps irreparably. My pulse was racing as fast as my engine when from the back seat came a sweet, totally laid-back "Hello, Mommy."

It was *her* doctor appointment, but, of course, at two years of age, what did she care about being late? Suddenly I was glad my hurry and stress had not rubbed off on her that morning. She was happy, relaxed, delighted just to spend the morning with Mommy. Could we say that here was the Lord in my child, helping me slow down?

A new superhighway has been completed just outside my office. I can get on it about one mile from my house and zoom efficiently to work in just under seven minutes. One day I drove to a lunchtime appointment across town, which took me past our church. Our church meets in a lovely old remodeled home, and had a row of stately maple trees along the front of the lot.

Suddenly I realized the trees were all gone, cut to the ground. A pain shot through my heart that day as though someone had knifed it. That sounds overly dramatic, but the pain was real. Then I recalled that the trees had been removed to make room for more superhighway. I was struck by my own inconsistency: four lanes were great as long as they took trees and yard from someone else.

New trees will be planted, of course. And just as surely, I suppose, little girls will someday hurry with all the fury of their harried mother. They will learn that if they're late for school, they'll collect tardy points and face the scowl of a teacher—later a boss. They will learn to speed on superhighways and snap at their children.

But I also hope I am teaching them to stop at a park on a day full of errands and spend thirty minutes at the playground. I hope they're learning that dishes will wait—but a sunset won't. That growing flowers in a garden makes pulling weeds worthwhile and that taking a walk is good Sunday afternoon medicine.

We can't escape a certain amount of fast-lane living. But we *can* make choices to tame the hurry in us. We can take five deep breaths at stoplights instead of letting the tension rise. We can turn off the TV a half hour early to make time to talk to a spouse or children or to read. We can go sledding with the kids, and have hot chocolate later, or simply enjoy a little roughhousing on the floor. We can get up ten minutes early to spend precious moments in solitude, talking with God to help control the hurry of the day. That will help us see God all day long, even when the kids are struggling to make the bus.

～§

VERSES FOR REFLECTION

"Martha, Martha," the Lord answered, "you are worried and upset about many things, but only one thing is needed. Mary has chosen what is better, and it will not be taken away from her."
Luke 10:41-42

The Latest
Trend

IT WAS ONE OF those statements that seem wise and psychologically sound but when you stop and think about them are just plain silly.

Our two-year-old needed tubes in her ears for chronic ear infections. For a child, this requires an outpatient hospital procedure under anesthesia. While coming out of the anesthesia she was crying, moaning, feeling awful like you feel when caught in that land between consciousness and unconsciousness.

"She'll be all right, Momma," said a kind and well-meaning nurse as I attempted to comfort Doreen.

Doreen kept on crying.

"She's just mad; she mostly feels insulted; the only one she feels safe to take her anger out on is you, Momma." She implied that once Doreen got the anger out of her system, she'd be all right.

I wished this woman who was old enough to be *my*

mother would stop calling me "Momma." But aside from that, I smiled vaguely, recognizing the "anger" idea from some ancient psychology text I'd studied. I didn't think about it too much more.

After Doreen had thrown up and felt good enough to start eating dry crackers, I started realizing how inane the advice really was. Doreen wasn't angry—at Momma, the doctor, or anyone else. She was just feeling rotten because of the anesthesia. Once she got *that* out of her system, she was soon as good as new.

How quickly we succumb to the god of the latest trend. And I'm the worst of the lot. If somebody tells me playing Beethoven for my child in the womb will make her a musician, I rush to plant headphones on my abdomen. (No, I didn't, but I've done things as outrageous.)

If career advisers tell us we've got to network to advance our careers, we join every imaginable club or lunch bunch and spread business cards like litter.

If the trend is spiritual retreats with a spiritual adviser, we schedule them in our appointment books—forgetting that a good old-fashioned day in the woods could serve the same purpose.

One family counselor said she can always tell what has been discussed on TV talk shows in a particular week because her patients all have whatever problem was featured on the shows!

I'm not really knocking good psychology or listening to classical music while pregnant or networking or taking spiritual retreats. It's just that too often we rush to adopt the latest trend without saying, "Wait a minute! What's really going on here?" Why would I rather network than call it what it is: promotion of me or my business? Why do I think my children have to be classical musicians? Why is it more comforting to think my child is crying because he's got to work out his anger than because he feels lousy after an operation? Why is it okay to say, "I have an appointment with my spiritual adviser," but not "This is my hour to be alone with God"?

"Vanity, vanity," said the writer of Ecclesiastes long ago, "All is vanity. There is nothing new under the sun" (Eccles. 1:2-9 paraphrased). That writer, after pursuing all of that day's current trends, ended up overwhelmingly pessimistic except for this good news: "The purpose of life is to eat and drink and find satisfaction in one's work—this is the gift of God" (Eccl. 2: 24, paraphrased).

It's comforting to know that God is everlasting. The New Age movement or even "spirituality" may be trends, but God is not subject to "in" and "out" lists. God just is.

❧

VERSE FOR REFLECTION
In the beginning was the Word, and the Word was with God,
and the Word was God. He was with God
in the beginning.
John 1:1

Living Our Gratitude

OUR PROBLEMS WERE minor compared to many people's, yet the combination of having a new baby put back in the hospital for jaundice, new-mother tiredness, and having two preschoolers to look after left me with few coping resources. Plus the two-year-old had suffered a seizure just four days before the baby was born, so the doctor wanted to run tests to determine the cause.

All of which meant extra expenses in addition to diminished energy.

A wonderful woman from our church volunteered to babysit so I could take our two-year-old for one of the tests. When I picked up the children after the appointment, Connie stuffed an envelope into the diaper bag, saying, "Someone came by and left this for you."

I couldn't wait until I got home to see what was in the envelope, but I did wait until we were in the car, driving down the street. With one hand I pulled out the plain envelope. In it was a crisp $100 bill.

You can imagine the tears, flowing so freely I could barely drive. *Who and why?* I wondered, while trying to explain to the girls that my tears were happy tears, that someone had just given us a lot of money. I felt like God had been snooping in my diaper bag.

Most of us have been recipients of someone's generosity at one time or another. We go through a difficult time of being without work or moving or needing an operation. People bring us food or money, do the laundry, provide transportation.

We feel so undeserving; how can we ever repay all the people who have helped?

We may never be able to repay the exact people who have helped us when we've needed a hand, but there are countless opportunities to turn around and spread the generosity to others. Being in need somehow makes us more aware of the needs of others and teaches us how to live out our gratitude.

I recently heard the story of a young volunteer in Central America. He had two jackets. One was a brand-new one his mother had given him, a special gift he really liked.

A Nicaraguan friend pointed out, "You have two jackets; I don't have any."

Dave gave him his newest jacket. Later he found out the "friend" had taken the jacket and sold it for a leather jacket.

Such stories anger us and provide fuel for arguments against aid for poor people. While we can be discerning and use good judgment in who and how we help, God also calls us just to respond to need and let recipients be accountable for their own actions.

Even when we give to established organizations rather than beggars on the street, most times there is no way to know whether they use it for the advertised need—or whether they use it for a "leather jacket." The organization may have sizable overhead. Even though we know all organizations need someone to pay for lights and paper clips, we'd rather have *our* donations go for milk and meat. Although we shouldn't put strings on our gifts, it's a good idea to use discretion in choosing which groups we give to.

When Michelle was four, she thought we could run to the bank and get more money anytime. She knew we got money out of the bank but didn't quite understand what it takes to put money in.

Similarly, when we make deposits of money and time to help other people, we are putting in something to draw on when we need it. At least I've found that to be true in the community that surrounds us. What a cause for thanksgiving, one more way I find God speaking in ordinary events.

⋥

VERSES FOR REFLECTION

I tell you the truth, this poor widow has put more into
the treasury than all the others. They all
gave out of their wealth; but she, out
of her poverty, put in everything—
all she had to live on.
Mark 12:43-44

Spiderweb

T HE DESK IN MY OFFICE once faced an ugly assortment of air-conditioning and heating units on an annex. Then I discovered that the simple act of turning the desk around would keep me from seeing the unsightly rooftop. Instead I could see trees, nearby houses, and a distant softball field.

But after my desk was turned around, I noticed for the first time that a spider had been weaving an unsightly web outside my windowpane. Never having been a big fan of spiders, I wondered how I could get rid of it since my office is on the second floor and the windows are sealed for climate control.

Then one day I noticed the spider struggling, trying to eat a fly caught by her web. I crept closer to watch the fight and was surprised to find dozens of tiny gnats snared by the web.

Instantly the spider was my friend. Harmless and safely out of my room, she was providing a wonderful service by putting gnats out of commission.

So often we respond to abrasive persons as I did to

the spider, failing to see any good they might be doing. The bully in school. The know-it-all at work. The relative who loudly airs political and social views at every reunion. We want to quiet them, get them out of our way, wish away their existence.

Then one day I noticed my spider friend and her home had just *gone*, washed away like so many other homes by the rains and wind from hurricanes or floods. It made me think of homelessness, an issue so much in the news that people have tired of the stories. To many, the homeless are unsightly.

What is it about homelessness that raises the dander, gets people going? Is it racism? Is it our pull-yourselves-up-by-the-bootstraps legacy? Is it fear that, in the space of a couple missed paychecks, the people in the homeless shelter could be us? Is it the memory of times we tried to help and someone took advantage of us?

Homelessness has many causes, including mental or physical disabilities which make it difficult to hold a job, poor money management, low-paying jobs, poverty after a divorce, the rebuilding of inner cities (raising rents in the process) and laziness, to name a few.

But we sometimes forget that there are also many reasons those of us with homes can afford our homes. The list could include hard work, cheating others, skillful money management, tax evasion, a windfall inheritance, wise investment, and gambling.

What's needed is a simple turnaround like occurred in my office, so we can look at things another way. Perhaps you'll see a spider—a sometimes unloved advocate for the homeless toiling selflessly at a thankless, endless task. Perhaps you'll find people caught in a web of bad luck beyond their control. Perhaps you'll see yourself: looking on from a position of safety when others are flushed from their homes through natural or economic disaster. Perhaps you'll see even the face of God. Jesus, we must remember, was homeless and warned his followers they wouldn't have a place to lay their heads.

There are no simple answers, but plain old courtesy and compassion can begin to bridge the widening rift between the haves and the have-nots. Finding ways to give voice and power to the voiceless is an additional starting point. Motivating others where motivation has died is another. Surely you'll think of more ideas, if you have the courage to look into the face of God.

෧෫

VERSE FOR REFLECTION

I tell you the truth, whatever you
did for one of the least of
these. . . , you did for me.
Matthew 25:40

Lessons from Digging a Well

T HE FIRST CUP OF WATER from our own well looked as welcome as an oasis in a desert. It made me think of people in some far-off country celebrating the completion of a village well; I suddenly felt a kinship with them.

But why the big deal? People dig wells every day in North America.

We had survived more weekends than I care to count without water. In Virginia many homes have cisterns instead of wells—holding tanks dug in the ground which collect water off the roofs of houses or buildings. A pump carries the water up into normal plumbing pipes. And yes, we actually drank the stuff (many still do.)

Anyway, we sometimes had waterless weekends because we'd forget to check the water in the cistern in time on Friday afternoon to buy a load of water before higher weekend rates went into effect.

In addition to the times we simply forgot to check the

water level, there were days of cistern cleaning (and no water), cistern re-plastering (a week without water), and the weekend there was a new baby in the house (with no water). It hardly qualified for genuine suffering but definitely rated as giant inconvenience.

We finally decided to take the plunge and dig a well. I doubt we'd have started if we'd known how deep we'd need to go. My husband was hoping to hit water by 250 feet but pessimistically predicted 500 feet at the most.

By the time we hit 600 feet, co-workers' jokes about oil and China were getting stale. We begged the driller to try another hole, but he wanted to go on. As the droning rig bore into the ground, it became a corkscrew impaling not only our budget but our nerves as well.

My husband checked by phone at every coffee break. "No water, at 725 feet," I'd report. "Still nuthin' at 800 feet." At night I read about Jacob's well-digging ventures in the Old Testament and suddenly felt a new respect for his patience with those well robbers (Gen. 26:17-22).

I didn't feel right praying that we'd find water. That seemed like praying for a boy or a girl after the baby's already been conceived! Enough faith may move mountains, but I didn't want to worry God about personal stream moving. Yet I *did* pray for patience to survive frayed nerves and peace not to worry about our stretched budget.

We drilled all the way to 925 feet. And finally we had water, almost twice as far down as our most pessimistic prediction. To my family, living where thirty- to ninety-foot wells are the norm, 925 feet went beyond ridiculous to ludicrous! How would we ever pay for it?

My husband talked to the contractor, who agreed to charge us for only 580 feet—the depth where we had urged him to try another hole. God hadn't moved a stream but maybe had softened a contractor's heart in compassion for a young, financially struggling family.

That wasn't the only lesson our well taught me, though. I was celebrating our new well when I read that in Ethiopia "in 75 percent of the households under survey, women spent three hours on a single journey to collect water." In India, water is often carried five miles each way, several times a day, in thousands of villages. All of this is in addition to cutting and carrying firewood, doing field work nine to ten hours a day, watching children, cooking, cleaning, doing hand laundry, and on and on (*Daughters of Sarah*, June 1984).

The woman in Samaria in John 4 who met Jesus at the well—one of Jacob's original wells!—was collecting water much as many women still do. She was looking, of course, for regular, earthly water. But Jesus gave her words that led her to eternal water and life.

When we used to go without water for a weekend, I always promised myself not to take the beauty of running water for granted again. Yet in a few days I'd be running and wasting it without even thinking about what a wonderful convenience it was.

Try this experiment with me: every time you do the very ordinary act of turning on a tap, think of persons walking miles for water. Think of the woman at the well who had such a desperate need for a new source of life. Experience the extraordinary water of eternal life flowing to you from God, the giver of love and grace.

ஒ

VERSES FOR REFLECTION
Everyone who drinks this water will be thirsty again, but whoever drinks the water I give . . . will never thirst. Indeed, the water I give . . . will become . . . a spring of water welling up to eternal life.
John 4:13-14

What Ever Happened to a Day of Rest?

"WHAT EVER HAPPENED to recess?" was a headline that caught my eye in the trade magazine of the advertising industry, *Advertising Age*.

Do you remember rushing out of school to a wide open playground to be the first on the monkey bars? Or to quickly choose sides for a ten-minute game of kick ball? For ten or twenty minutes, you forgot about math, English, and social studies, then came back in smelling like fresh air, dirt, and sweat.

Children today know too little of recess. In elementary school, we got three recesses a day—morning, lunch, and afternoon. But maybe that's a topic for another book. Maybe kids have less recess because the adults around them fail to take advantage of a one-day-a-week recess.

I grew up as a deacon's daughter, when we had well-defined rules about what you could or couldn't do on Sundays. Washing dishes (which I hated), was okay, but working on a sewing project (which I loved) was not. Gathering eggs was okay because it was a necessary evil on our poultry farm, but sorting the eggs was not okay. That waited until Monday.

I remember thinking of Sundays in legalistic terms. I believed keeping all the rules would somehow earn me a better berth in heaven. Even though I no longer feel bound by legalism, I am grateful that keeping a day of rest was so deeply ingrained in me. Finally, I can think of the sixth commandment in freeing terms: "Honor the Sabbath day to keep it holy" means I don't have to feel guilty for curling up with a good book on Sunday afternoon instead of washing windows!

Sabbath means literally "a time of rest." In today's society, many people *have* to work on Sunday. For pastors Sundays are often the most hectic day of the week. Therefore, anyone needing to work regularly on Sundays is wise to make another day *different*, a day of relaxation.

I was upset when our city gave up ancient blue laws to permit any business to open on Sunday. I'm still upset, but on a few occasions have sneaked into a discount store or the mall—looking furtively over my shoulder in hopes no one I knew would see me there. I've been surprised at the numbers I see there. Are they all like me, I wonder, making an exception because of a last-minute birthday party? I also wonder at my own inconsistencies—we think nothing of buying gas or eating out on Sunday. Why does it feel different to go to the mall?

I wonder if my children will think twice about going to the mall on Sunday when they grow up. If not, I do hope they still allow a day of rest in their schedules—a day when they don't feel pressured to work in the garden or do work from the office.

Occasionally we may need to make exceptions, such as throwing a load of clothes in the washer because the kids are out of clean underwear. Didn't Jesus speak to that when he said, "The Sabbath was made for [humans], not [humans] for the Sabbath" (Mark 2:27)? That means that humans should be free to pursue good, worthwhile, helpful activities on their day of rest. What's work to me may not be work to you.

I remember one Sunday afternoon in the flatlands of north Florida where I lived in 1969. Father heard a truck roaring from forward to reverse, trying to rock out of the mud. Dad had no idea who it was but threw a heavy chain on his tractor and went to see if he could help.

The man happened to be a schoolteacher of mine, notorious for his dislike of hypocritical Christians. On Monday morning I sat in Mr. Finlay's class. A great story-teller, he told in great detail how he had been out hunting, got stuck, and was terribly relieved to see my dad putting across the fields to the rescue.

"I know Mr. Miller is a Christian who doesn't believe in working on Sunday. I couldn't believe he would get on his tractor and take the risk of people thinking he was 'working.' Tell your dad thanks for me again, Melodie."

Making one day out of seven a rest day was probably one of the best things God could have planned for us. In mental health literature, much is made of the need for relaxation and recreation—taking care of yourself. It can be a special time to see God.

✎

VERSE FOR REFLECTION

And God blessed the seventh day and made it holy, because on it he rested from all the work of creating.
Genesis 2:3

Grace on the Road

S TOPPED BY A COP and accused of stealing $1 worth of watermelons, daughter throwing up the first mile away from home, husband down with flu the first twelve hours —all the makings of a miserable vacation.

While packing the car, coming off a day of flu myself and knowing the daughter and husband didn't feel too hot, I told myself, *Some people would say, "Oh let's just stay home."*

I'm glad I'm not "some people," even though over the years I've come to realize how difficult travel sometimes is—even just a one-day attempt at getting away.

I remember climbing down a seventy-five-degree cliff with my husband to get to a swimming hole with three children (a five-year-old, a three-year-old, and a six-month-old) plus all of their gear. After thinking, "If Mom could see me now," I laughed out loud at the absurdity of the scene.

Travel, although pleasant and mind-expanding, can certainly be filled with times of pure misery. When people talk about the planes they missed or how long they had to circle O'Hare Airport, I can never tell if they're bragging or complaining!

The day we were accused of stealing $1 worth of melons happened to be a Sunday morning when we were traveling home from the beach. We had just finished a mini-worship service in the car when my husband saw the trooper's light come on behind him.

Apparently when we had stopped at a roadside stand a half hour earlier, the attendant thought we had stashed more melons in the back of the station wagon than we had paid for. So she had alerted the police. After a brief search by a somewhat embarrassed officer, he sent us on our way.

No matter what difficulties may arise, hope springs eternal for vacations where everything goes better than planned, where we find a needed change of pace and time for renewal.

More and more people use vacations as a time to expand family interests and hobbies and to pass on certain values. I was pleased to learn of Arthur Frommer's (of *Europe on $5 a Day* fame) new emphasis on going beyond sightseeing vacations. His new book, *The New World of Travel*, emphasizes such alternative travel possibilities as volunteer work vacations, study vacations, and living with families in other countries.

My parents did this long before Frommer started writing about it. One of my earliest memories is of our family spending two vacation weeks teaching summer Bible school at a church on Troublesome Creek in eastern Kentucky.

Even on regular vacations my parents were especially good at seeking out churches of our denomination—no sleeping in on a Sunday morning for the Miller family! Whether we found ourselves in Pea Ridge, Missouri, Niagara Falls, or Downey, California, we got out the Sunday dresses and trotted off to strange Sunday school classes.

We took part in work camps and visited the voluntary service units of our denomination—groups of mostly young people doing community or hospital work for one or two years. They made church service look like fun and whetted my appetite to someday join them.

Now when I hear of a church in Timbuktu, Montana, I can picture the tiny, homey congregation and remember the venison we had for Sunday dinner at the pastor's house. Weeks at church camps introduced us to a variety of leaders and speakers, names still special to me today.

I don't mean my parents were pious Joes who turned every family trip into a religious experience. Rather they believed that one's religion never took a vacation. As the occasion arose, tracking down a new church was as much a part of a family trip as trying out new restaurants and roadside attractions. To be honest, we may have grumbled about hardly ever getting to sleep in on a Sunday morning, but as parents are fond of predicting, I'm thankful now.

Certainly there's place for a restful week at the beach or hitting the highlights of a city like Toronto. There's place for a wide variety of experiences. But thoughtful travelers can ask themselves, *What values am I passing on in my choice of vacation spots?*

✑

VERSE FOR REFLECTION
But Mary treasured up all these things and
pondered them in her heart.
Luke 2:19

Dinner-Plate
Dahlias

A UNT MAE'S HOME was tucked at the very end of a mountain hollow, the term folks use to describe the V-shaped winding pass in and through low-lying Appalachian mountains. Flowers—annuals and perennials alike—grew in every smidgen of spare dirt at Aunt Mae's place, and in every old pot or pan she could put to that use.

A long-stemmed gourd hung on the wall of a shed, a woodbox on the porch held fuel for the kitchen cookstove; a well-kept outhouse sat a discreet distance from the house. There was even an old, natural spring with a cupboard built over the top. Wild ferns and potted wandering Jews placed artfully around the spring made it more than just a place to draw drinking water: it looked like a place to find the kind of "living water" Jesus offered to the woman at the well.

In late summer, the impatiens spread out like small

bushes, coleus flourished in dark greens and rich reds, and dinner-plate dahlias grew as big as their name predicts.

Aunt Mae and Uncle George raised chickens for a living until technology shut them out of the increasingly competitive poultry world. They could not afford to make the improvements on their poultry house required by the producer with whom they contracted. Taking care of chickens keeps you close to home—family reunions used to be planned around "when George's chickens are sold." That way Mae and George wouldn't have to worry about electrical storms turning off the fans in the chicken house on a sweltering August Sunday.

Of course, there was much about my husband's aunt I really didn't know. When she succumbed to cancer at the not-so-old age of sixty-eight, I wondered if Aunt Mae was happy back that long lane, a mile from the nearest road, eighteen miles from the nearest town. How could any one living in our time be happy with as little as Aunt Mae had?

At her funeral in a little knotty pine church, the sanctuary was full; I didn't know she even knew so many people. But that was my ignorance. At the dinner held after her funeral, I puttered around her yard, breathing in the beauty and tranquility of what a real estate ad might call "a mountain Eden." I decided Aunt Mae *must* have been happy, if flowers and friends and family and faith in God can fill one with joy.

I'm sure she had her disappointments like all of us, and great frustration in battling cancer over several years and numerous operations. But one lesson I'm trying to absorb from Aunt Mae is her apparent joy in the simple things of life.

It's not wrong to have big visions, to have great ideas about what you want to accomplish and dreams for your children. But so often goals and aspirations—our dreams of "making it big"—block out real appreciation for all that we already enjoy.

There was a nice but not extravagant number of flower arrangements lining the entrance to the church at her funeral. There were probably more store-bought flowers than Aunt Mae had ever received in her life, but somehow the luxury seemed appropriate. How else would you celebrate the life of this green thumb than by offering up lots of beautiful bouquets? Flowers ask so little of life; they just make the world a prettier place during their short existence.

Do you know any "Aunt Maes"? You know, those saints whose main gift to the world was that they taught others how to appreciate life, and maybe know a little more of God?

‹•§

VERSES FOR REFLECTION

Do not store up for yourselves treasures on earth, where moth
and rust destroy, and where thieves break in and steal.
But store up for yourselves treasures in heaven,
where moth and rust do not destroy, and
where thieves do not break in and steal.
For where your treasure is, there
your heart will be also.
Matthew 6:19-21

Late Bloomer

K INDERGARTEN KIDS are famous for bringing home cups full of dirt and scraggly growing things for Mother's Day. The year Tanya brought home a fairly hardy (considering the bus trip) marigold plant, we dutifully reset the marigold outdoors and watched for the first bloom.

But the little marigold just sat there, not dying but certainly not thriving; it didn't bloom all summer long. It was a summer of great rains in our part of the country, and I began to wonder if too *much* moisture was the problem. Maybe we had poor soil, or too much shade, or who knows what. Other flowers in the same bed did fairly well. But the marigold just sat there reminding me that I really don't have much of a green thumb.

Toward the end of an unseasonably warm October, I began to notice a small bud forming. And on November 1 (which I consider the first day of winter no matter what the calendar says) Tanya's little marigold was finally blooming. I happened to need a fresh flower greeting me that day.

If it had bloomed on schedule, no one would have

made much of it. But as it was, I called Tanya to celebrate.

No matter how old you are, are there goals you've dreamed of achieving all your life but never had the time to work on? Why wait for the right time to get started? Cemeteries are filled with people who were waiting for the right time.

A thirty-one-year-old woman decided what she'd really like to be was a doctor. "But I can't go to school now. I'd be forty before I got through!"

"And what will you be in nine years if you *don't* follow your dream?" a wise friend asked.

The woman decided to go for it.

So what if you didn't get the vocational training you wanted in high school? It may be more difficult now, with two kids and a mortgage, but people are doing it all the time. So what if you haven't pursued the art or drama or writing you'd like to? Look into possibilities today.

The young artist, the guy who makes a million before he's twenty-five, the child prodigy—all these are plentiful. To be a late bloomer, to be a Grandma Moses, to learn to swim when you're in your eighties as one woman did—well, there's something special about that.

You may never become well known, rich, or an Olympic champion. To be honest, that marigold blooming in November was no raving beauty; it was always puny and bedraggled. Yet the miracle to me was that it produced at all—late and unspectacular but accomplishing the purpose for which it was put on this earth.

Persons who have near-death experiences or survive serious illness often say, "I guess Somebody has a reason for me to still be here." And often they live with awareness of the miracle of greeting another day.

I hope you'll let my marigold story remind you that there's still time to begin working on a goal you wanted to accomplish. *Today* I can be more organized, tidy, or free-spirited (if that's my need). *Today* I can make that call or write a letter to inquire about a new class, school, or job. *Today* I can make a fresh start in my relationship with God and work on improving relationships with those around me.

Richard Foster (in *Money, Sex and Power*) suggests that real Christianity comes in the small day-to-day deeds. We are often looking to do great things, but the story of the widow's mite (Luke 21:1-4) would indicate the small deeds and the attitudes of the heart is where Christianity is lived out.

⋖⋗

VERSES FOR REFLECTION

He also saw a poor widow put in two very small copper coins.
"I tell you the truth," he said, "this poor widow
has put in more than all the others."
Luke 21:2-3

Discarded Bouquets

O NE DAY I CAME across a cleaning woman in a college campus bathroom.

Nothing so unusual about that. Bathrooms are usually where we find cleaning women (and sometimes men). We usually go our way without pausing to thank or even notice them as persons. In fact, I think we try *not* to recognize them as persons because then we don't have to deal with the fact that real people clean up our dribbled toilets and casually tossed tissues.

But this woman was not, at the moment, cleaning. She was painstakingly rescuing a discarded bouquet of flowers—picking out the old, faded blossoms, and rearranging the remaining blooms into a still-decent bouquet.

"Rescuing some flowers?" I said as I washed my hand, never one to shine in the "Bright and Original Comments in Spontaneous Situations" department.

"Yeah," she sighed, "they'll probably only last another day, or maybe by evening they'll be gone, but . . ." She left the sentence unfinished, hanging like the future of the flowers.

I guessed that as she was going about her normal business of cleaning offices, she had found the slightly frumpy flowers and on her own had decided to try to help them brighten someone's office for one more day. Perhaps some would fault her for using company time for the task. And while I don't want to make too big a deal of it, I was impressed by the love and hope embodied in that simple act of rearranging a half-spent bouquet. She was God's messenger to me that day.

So many things in life are like that cleaning woman rescuing those flowers. We put energy, enthusiasm, and love into raising our children but have no guarantees about the outcome. Thousands of persons even go the second mile, raising the children of *other* people in foster care programs. Foster children have often fallen through the cracks and depend entirely on the love and dedication of foster parents who pick them up, scrub them off, and do their best to put them back on their feet.

I think of those working with AIDS patients. At present there is so little reason to hope, and like one AIDS patient said, "The good that is coming out of all of this is that people are learning simply to love people because they are people and they hurt."

Some people would like to discard persons with AIDS in some trash basket in a deserted rest room. When confronted with AIDS on a personal basis, most of us have a lot of fear and hysteria to process. Yet we can't help but feel, intuitively, that if Jesus were here, he would be in there, touching and teaching, regardless of personal cost.

A third group I admire are those working with persons who have mental and physical disabilities. Nearby we have a group home for differently-abled adults; many attend our church on Sunday morning. I watch the workers patiently and constantly reminding these adults of rudimentary manners—to keep demonstrations of affection in check, to not talk out loud. In short, they are being taught to behave as other adults do. I marvel at the rescue of life that others would discard and keep safely hidden behind four walls.

Too often we have assumed that it's not worth the effort to teach good manners to persons with disabilities. The presence of our friends from Harrison House in worship has more than once touched me in ways no sermon could have. For instance, the day Janet formally joined our church, she was so eager with her "Yes, yes, yes," to the traditional questions asked of church members that I was left wondering why we couldn't all be so enthusiastic about membership. These friends are flowers well worth the rescuing (if the metaphor is not offensive).

If we look around us, there are many "flowers" waiting to be rescued; maybe a truant child everyone else has given up on; maybe an adult who wants to learn to read; maybe a couple ready to give up on marriage. All it takes is the cleaning woman's vision that someone or something is worth rescuing for even one more day.

❧

VERSES FOR REFLECTION
See how the lilies of the field grow. They do not labor or spin. Yet I tell you that not even Solomon in all his splendor was dressed like one of these.
Matthew 6:28b-29

Morning Glories

I S A MORNING GLORY a flower or a weed?
"Weed," says my husband. "Look how it takes over the garden."

"Flower!" say the children. "The babysitter plants morning glories by her fence post."

Of course, they're both partly right in the half-truths that make up most arguments. As usual, I waffle. When a morning glory volunteered in my flower bed last year, I trained it around the edge of the flower bed. When one crops up in the corn, I yank it out with little sympathy.

Toward the end of August our garden seems mostly taken over with weeds much less attractive than morning glories. It is nice to get to this time of year, when you don't have to really care how the garden looks, and just feel happy about the produce to be found among the weeds. At the end of August, if your garden is still as neat as my father-in-law's, you've probably reached the stage in life when gardening can be truly a hobby and not something you somehow squeeze in.

Actually I do enjoy gardening when I have the time.

Gardening offers so many metaphors for life. When I'm weeding the garden in early summer, I always think that tending a garden is like working on a marriage: you have to take care of the little problems as they crop up before they grow huge and unwieldy.

Now that fall is approaching and the weeds have grown unmanageable (somewhere between vacations and other duties, I gave up), I compare the garden to the aging process. In the youthfulness of spring, we set out eager every year to have the best garden ever. Great plans. No weeds. New varieties. A showcase flower bed. Just like an upstart young graduate with great plans to change the world.

As the summer wears on, the duties of tending for plants conflict with *harvesting* the crops. If I have a choice between pulling weeds in the corn and *picking* the corn for supper or to freeze, the picking will win every time. So it is with the person in middle life; beginning to enjoy the fruits of our labors a bit, we go a little easier on the disciplines. If I have the choice of having a perfectly clean house for company or spending the afternoon at the pool with the children, I'll compromise on the housework and go for the fun.

As fall sets in, the garden doesn't look so pretty anymore, but my freezer is full again and fresh cans of beans and tomatoes sit on my pantry shelves. In fall when I go to the garden, I'm just happy to find a good tomato or be delighted with beans that started to produce again. We laboriously pick through corn on the cob that has half succumbed to worms. I suppose that's a little like the "golden years" although I wouldn't presume to speak for anyone. You feel good about the fruits of your labors and concentrate more on enjoying the grandchildren rather than *raising* them.

But back to the morning glories. I guess the thing I

like about the morning glory is that no matter how with-ered it looks the night before, in the morning it opens again, vibrant and full of life. This daily coming and go-ing, this daily chance to shine and "glory" is certainly the way I view each day; no matter how depressed or sad or tired I am at day's end, by morning I usually feel like a new person. I guess that's because I'm basically a morn-ing person, and things always look better to me in the morning.

The morning glory—whether you call it weed or flower—reminds me that most of life is best taken one day at a time. If you're down, remember you only have to get through this day. If you're up, remember you may only *have* this day, so live it thoroughly. Like the morning glory, we can revel in the magic of being revived for each new day! Like the old hymn says, "I owe the Lord a morn-ing song, of gratitude and praise; for the kind mercy he has shown in length'ning out my days."

◦§

VERSE FOR REFLECTION

For his anger lasts only a moment, but his favor lasts
a lifetime; weeping may remain for a night,
but rejoicing comes in the morning.
Psalm 30:5

Confessions of
an Addict

I GET UP, GROPE FOR SLIPPERS, and soon pump fresh caffeine into my veins. Am I any different from the heroin addict, except that what I do is legal?

Oh, I've tried to kick the habit a number of times—going cold turkey, gradual withdrawal, decaffeination, herbal teas—I've tried a lot of ways. I'd stay clean and be self-righteous about it for several weeks, then I'd splurge at a friend's house or restaurant. And I did manage to quit caffeine during three pregnancies, since they say pregnant women who drink a lot of coffee have babies with lower birth weights.

When one of our children was about fifteen months old and struggling to give up her bottle, I chuckled as I watched a grown man nurse a beer bottle with two hands one day at an archery competition. He looked so much like my toddler, attached to his "security."

Then in a flash I saw myself, walking around the office

or at home, coffee cup clutched between two hands.

From time to time I teach college writing. One student wrote a paper about the innocence of marijuana and how it should be legalized. Although I didn't agree with him, I was hard put to condemn him. For while I sat there grading his paper, I was trying to keep myself awake for the dozen more papers I needed to grade with, you guessed it: a cup of high-octane coffee.

Am I really saying there is no difference between coffee and marijuana, beer, or worse substances? Of course there is, but my coffee habit helps me at least glimpse the power more harmful drugs can have.

Caffeine is psychologically addicting. I owned up to this the weekend some years ago when budget cutbacks (the *private,* not federal kind!) forced me to go an entire two days without coffee. We had only $10 left for groceries, and I couldn't spare $2 for a bag of coffee, so I would just have to do without until I got to the office Monday morning. I felt real, genuine, horrible panic. The fact that I felt panic made me feel even worse!

I am also convinced that one's body can become physically addicted to caffeine. For a year I lived in Spain and was served strong coffee—although liberally laced with milk—every morning *except* Sunday. My roommates and I often ended up with severe headaches on Sunday. Is it any wonder caffeine is combined with aspirin in certain headache medications?

So why do I keep on drinking coffee?

On a bus trip one time I noticed that one passenger ate by herself when we took a meal break. I went over to her afterward and said "I'm sorry you had to eat by yourself."

"Oh, I wouldn't inflict this on anyone else," she said, nodding in the direction of her cigarette.

I shrugged, admiring her honesty and said, "Well, I

guess I'm the same way with coffee," and after a few more minutes of conversation, I felt I'd gained a friend.

I wish I could say I'd given up my crutch. That would be the perfect end to this meditation. That would make all the coffee drinkers feel guilty and the nondrinkers smug. I believe I could do it if I really wanted to; I have quit/abstained from other habits. I guess the bottom line is that I'm not ready to.

Meanwhile, it makes me a little more sympathetic toward alcoholics, foodaholics, chain smokers, and addicts on the street. It helps me see myself as God sees us: there is no hierarchy of sins.

Is it time to make some change? What can I learn from my own weaknesses which will help me be more understanding of others? How can I live a lifestyle that is healthy and pleasing to God?

※

VERSE FOR REFLECTION

For by the grace given me I say to every one of you: Do not think of yourself more highly than you ought, but rather think of yourself with sober judgment, in accordance with the measure of faith God has given you.
Romans 12:3

Of Tomato Skins
and Such

ARE YOU A TOMATO-SKIN PEELER or a tomato-skin eater?
I hate to peel tomatoes and I certainly don't mind
eating the skins. Furthermore, I suspect that as with
many other fruits or vegetables, more of the vitamins
hang around in the skins. Therefore, I prefer my tomatoes unpeeled.

But this world is made up of tomato-skin haters and
tomato-skin eaters. My husband is one of the former.

So when I took the pain to peel some tomatoes as a
special treat for my husband one day, I wasn't prepared
for our six-year-old's response. "Why did you peel these
tomatoes?" she demanded, as if I'd done something to
offend her on purpose. I dutifully explained that Daddy
likes them that way, to which she replied, "Well, I think
tomatoes hang together better with their skins on."

I couldn't have said it better myself.

Then a tomato-skin hater at the office explained that

she used to be an eater until she started peeling; now she thinks the skins are so tough she can hardly stand to eat them! So my husband wasn't just being difficult. I needed to be more tolerant.

Why carry on about tomato-skins? Simply because it reminds me again that the world is made up of people with differences ranging from trivial to "now this is something I would die for." It's not easy to get along with people who think differently than we do, even if the issue is trivial. How do we work through petty annoyances?

I solved the tomato skin problem in our family by employing the centuries-old art of compromise: on occasion I peel half the tomato, leaving the other half to "hang together better."

Would that all differences were so neatly solved! What do we do when two sides seem forever divided? How do we get along in families where Grandpa will never see politics my way?

Duane Sider, a pastor, speaker, and composer, has pointed out that unity always arises out of diversity. The feeling or spirit of unity arises from differences. First Corinthians 12:12 puts it this way: "The body is a unit, though it is made up of many parts; and though all its parts are many, they form one body." The word *unity* implies a bringing together of different parts. It implies differences. If everyone thought exactly alike we wouldn't call it unity, we'd call it unanimous. Or boring.

So differences can be healthy. Perhaps we could even say the world is a better place to live in because of people with differences. We all need each other.

But differences are also very frustrating and tragic; they are at the root of nearly every problem in the world. So while we celebrate differences on the one hand, we need to work to find every possible point of agreement on the other hand.

In North America we enjoy a society that on the surface tolerates everything from Moonies to old-world orthodox religions. One of the most cherished freedoms is the freedom to be different—to believe differently, to worship in the manner we choose. People seeking religious freedom sacrificed their livelihood and sometimes their lives as they moved to the New World. The freedom to be different is wonderful in theory but difficult to extend to our neighbors today.

God loves both the tomato-skin hater and the tomato-skin eater. Let us celebrate the diversity among us, even while holding fast to some beliefs we would die (but not kill) for.

If, as they say, the measure of my love for God is the same as the measure of my love for the person I like least, I have a long way to go in learning to appreciate diversity. When I'm bothered by someone's differentness, I can be reminded that God loves us equally.

VERSE FOR REFLECTION
The second is this: Love your neighbor as yourself. There is no commandment greater than these.
Mark 12:31

Turnaround

A T OUR OFFICE we used to have a cactus plant that bloomed about three or four times a year. I'm not a big fan of cacti, but there was something about this particular plant's blooming that always caught my imagination.

The flower, a feathery lilac bloom as delicate as any orchid, lasted only one day. It would burst open one morning and by evening was limp, exhausted and spent from its one brief shining.

One morning I came to work to find it was the cactus' day to bloom. But the flowers were squashed up against the window with no room to spread out. So I turned the planter around and watched the flowers unfold more fully. I imagined them thanking me for not having to spend their one day of glory bent up and miserable.

It made me think of a man I know, who in a sense spends his life turned in the wrong direction because of forces beyond his control when he was a child. I now believe he was damaged by a warped childhood, with no one to turn him around enough to say, "Look at life from

57

this side now. You don't have to wallow in the circumstances of your birth. You're free to become better than you've ever been before, given room to stretch and bloom." I no longer blame him for the hurtful ways he treats others, but I'd love to see him, even now in retirement, freed from some of his past.

In her book *Irregular People*, Joyce Landorf tells how we can cope with people who have "irregular" ways of relating to others—especially someone close to us at work or in the family whom we must see on a regular basis. First, attempt to understand a person's background, and find out what forces may have influenced his or her life.

Second, try to keep from developing unrealistic expectations about your relationship with that person. If you go to a holiday gathering expecting a miraculously picture-perfect family, you're sure to be crushed. You can *pray* for a changed heart and improved relationships, but don't let one person ruin your whole day.

Third, find ways to pour out your anger, guilt, and unresolved feelings, perhaps to a trusted friend. You'll probably find you need to ask God for forgiveness frequently, as it's so easy to give in to hateful feelings.

But, of course, all of this is much easier to write than do, even if we recognize the need to turn around. One mother was having difficulty relating to her fifth grade son, who seemed to push every wrong button in her. They were a lot alike, and he was so exasperating in his bookworm nature, his one-track mind, his on-and-on descriptions of his latest idea for something. She knew he was brilliant, but sometimes she didn't have the patience to live with brilliance.

One day she arrived at school to pick him up for a dentist appointment. She peeked through the window first and saw him at the teacher's desk. The teacher was obviously enjoying the boy and listening to him with shining eyes that said, "I really enjoy this kid."

Is there someone with whom I need to experience a turnaround? Who could give me a different perspective on that person? Sometimes prayer alone is enough to help me make a change. God can help me see others and with fresh insight. Perhaps I would do well to remember that the only one I can really change in a relationship is myself. How can I experience healing so *I* don't become warped in my outlook?

VERSES FOR REFLECTION
In those days John the Baptist came, preaching
in the Desert of Judea and saying, "Repent,
for the kingdom of heaven is near."
Matthew 3:1-2

Of Cops
and Quotas

MY WIFE WILL GET A TOASTER if I can just write two more speeding tickets this week," quipped the trooper when I asked him if police officers really had quotas to fill.

Of course, he was joking, affirming my suspicion that all the talk about quotas was mostly myth. "Our department has never had, to my knowledge, any kind of quota system," he continued more seriously.

"Oh, if one year my totals were really off from previous years, my supervisor might ask me what's going on." And I'm sure there's pressure to perform in all departments: pressure to do the job society has asked them to do but really doesn't want them to carry out. "But we have no set numbers," he concluded.

Maybe I'm naive to believe him, a Christian cop with a positive witness. These things have been on my mind lately because, you guessed it, I've been disobeying the law and I finally got my just deserts. If that way of putting it sounds strange to you, I'm not trying to sound "holier than thou" here. I'm trying to make us think about the language we use when we talk about cops and speeding tickets. We laugh in triumph when the other guy gets pulled over, but play the innocent victim when it's our turn.

"There's a police car," I warn my husband as we travel down the road, without thinking about the message I'm sending my children. Am I telling them it's okay to disobey the law as long as we don't get caught? That police officers are persons to be feared? Avoided? That *they're* the ones somehow doing something wrong by chasing innocent people?

Okay. Inwardly I did my share of complaining at having to pay a $71 fine. I was outraged that there I was, a mother with my three children and going home from a *church* meeting, no less, and his stopping me caused the two-year-old to wake up when I was hoping to just tuck her in bed when I got home. And besides, a twenty-five-mile-per-hour speed limit on that street was ridiculous. When had they changed it? (I later learned it had been that way for years, and that's why I say it was probably about time I was punished.)

The trooper who answered my question about quotas also shared quite frankly that for many years he wasn't a Christian because of the hypocrisy he saw as a police officer. "I almost got into a fight with a minister once because he claimed I couldn't ticket him as a minister of the gospel. I said, 'I'm sorry, but they didn't tell us that in basic training.' "

There is something about driving that reveals our true selves. I've been with otherwise fine, charming persons who turn into rude, lawbreaking slobs when they get behind a wheel. Stop signs aren't for stopping. They're for rolling through as we write our own rules going down the road. If I forget to put on my turn signal it's an innocent slip; if the other guy does, he's a stupid road hog. Grown-ups become childish revenge-seekers if someone follows too closely, forgets to dim headlights, or travels too slowly.

And okay, some police officers are gun-happy, vengeful characters who seem to gloat while writing us up. I'd guess they're a very small minority, but they unfortunately reinforce our stereotypes every time we hear about them.

The point is—and we forget it all too often as we hop in our cars to rush to our next destination—that the road is a dangerous place to be. Law enforcement officers generally help make life less dangerous. We worry about cancer and muggers and nuclear war, but the truth is that we come close to injury or death every time we get in the car. I don't mean to sound morbid or fatalistic; I just want to be more thoughtful myself when *I* take to the road. Can the highway be one more way to keep us more closely in touch with God?

える

VERSE FOR REFLECTION
Show me your ways, O Lord, teach me your paths.
Psalm 25:4

Picking Up
the Pieces

A POTTERY STUDENT in graduate school struggled all semester with a teacher, who for some reason, didn't seem to like anything she produced.

On the last day of class, the teacher picked up this student's final assignment. "Oh, you did this," said the teacher, and I'm sure the student thought maybe she had managed to make something the teacher liked.

In front of everyone, the teacher let the piece fall to the floor. It shattered.

This is a true story, sad to say, and the person who witnessed it said it was one of the "most heart rending things I've ever seen. I hope I never see it again."

While few of us would be so cruel as to drop someone's artwork on purpose, I'm afraid we all are guilty of shattering other people's spirits at times.

"Why did you buy another woodworking tool?" I ask my husband, who is always coming up with new projects. "You never finish anything anyway!"

"That's nice," I say about the kindergartner's latest painting, "but why is it all black?"

A new employee's idea for reducing paper use is shot down when the boss says, "But we always do it this way."

On the other hand, even a small word of encouragement can be enough to send a struggling student, spouse, or employee back to the drawing board with determination to do better.

Marriage therapists John and Naomi Lederach illustrate this need for affirmation by saying people are like barrels and we each have a dipper. As we go through life, people either help fill our barrel with affirmation, praise, and love, or they dip out of our barrel with criticism and put-downs.

Often people criticize out of a need to appear better themselves, but when we criticize unfairly or demean others, the level in our own barrel of good feelings goes down. On the other hand, when we praise and affirm others, our own self-esteem rises.

Naomi tells of seeing a boy and father at a discount store checkout counter. The boy wanted a soft drink. The father loudly and harshly told the boy, "No! You don't need one! And anyway, why don't you have your own money?"

Naomi says we've all seen these embarrassing scenarios; it may be helpful to recognize that the man's barrel was obviously very low, and he lashed out at the boy to make himself look better.

The good news is that often it only takes one person to begin to turn things around. If lashing out lowers the level in our barrels, then affirming others helps to fill up those empty, needy barrels. But it may take time.

Charles makes a dumb mistake—something we all do at times. After criticizing Charles, Sharon realizes that arguing about who was at fault won't prove anything, so she drops the matter. The next time they see each other she praises Charles for a kind deed she recently saw him do, and Charles mellows like an apple. The relationship is restored; Charles' barrel has been refilled and so has Sharon's.

Remember the Bible story of the prophet Elijah who asked a poor woman for water and bread? The woman said "I don't have any bread, only a handful of flour in a jar and a little oil in a jug."

Elijah said to her, "Don't be afraid. Make a small cake of bread for me from what you have, and then make something for yourself and your son. For God says, 'The jar of flour will not be used up and the jug of oil will not run dry.' " The woman did as she was told and was blessed with a continual supply of flour and oil.

Our jars will never run dry when we find ways to pour *genuine* encouragement and praise into the jars of others. Do you know someone with a low barrel today? Can you help someone else pick up the pieces of a shattered self-esteem and begin building on the good that is in everyone? If you can help someone else in this way, you are doing the work of God. You are God's hands, feet, and mouth in the world.

⋘§

VERSE FOR REFLECTION
A word aptly spoken is like apples
of gold in settings of silver.
Proverbs 25:11

Spare Me the Details

A N INTERVIEWER WAS TALKING to an elderly woman whose husband had been murdered several months earlier in an apparently random shooting. These lines come almost verbatim from a transcript of the interview.

"Do you remember your feelings during that period?" he asked, innocently pursuing the most interesting part of the story.

"Wait a minute," Mrs. Todd (not her real name) protested. "I wanted to tell you about our *marriage* before we got to this part. You got the book backward! You're asking me about his *death,* and you never thought of asking me about our lives together."

Ouch! To his credit, at that point the interviewer backed up and listened to a grieving woman remember her life with a wonderful husband.

How often do we tell people, by our attention or lack of it, "Just get on with the story; spare me the details." We want to know who won first prize, not who had fun creating a science fair exhibit. We want to know who got elected, not how tiring it was to campaign. We want to know if Mom got a promotion, not how many hours she worked for it. People read headlines but have less time for books.

That's why I was glad for Mrs. Todd's not-so-subtle reminder that people (and especially we in the media) have more time for sensation than sentiment.

I'm the same way at home. I ask the nursery schooler, "How did school go?" Then my mind wanders to what's cooking on the stove as she goes into some fanciful tale describing a "ghostbusters" game.

True, some people spend too much time describing details and end up asking, "Now what was I saying?" It *is* frustrating to be in a time bind and have to listen to whether Aunt Tilly was wearing pink or purple on the day in question. Some people live life in broad strokes; others need to pay attention to the particular curve of lip on a bemused Mona Lisa.

I took a still-life oil painting class once. Our teacher was always telling us, "Squint, squint, squint! See the lines around my eyes? They come from years of squinting! You have to squint to determine the exact shade of red in an apple, or the precise gleam on an oil lamp. You won't be a good painter if you don't squint!"

I like to remember her "Squint!" when I'm listening to my daughters or husband. (Funny how I have less trouble truly listening to my boss!) To squint—if not literally, at least figuratively—blocks out all the busy issues crowding my mind and lets me find out what's on another person's mind.

Details can mean all the difference between communication and understanding, or misunderstanding and hurt. Two co-workers at coffee break illustrate the point. Amy had lost a dog she was attached to in an accident but had since gotten another dog. By mistake Dora referred to the second dog by the first dog's name.

"I think you mean 'Tracey,'" Amy said helpfully. Dora was embarrassed she had forgotten. She walked away, mumbling that it was time to get back to work. Amy, on the other hand, thought Dora was mad at her for being corrected. They were both left with misunderstandings and mixed feelings about what had gone on.

Details, details! If we don't understand what point B has to do with point A, we'll usually get the connection if we listen long enough. More importantly, the person who is talking to us *feels* understood and knows someone cares when we listen with "squinting" ears. We need to listen between the lines and hear the unspoken as well as the spoken.

I like to think that God squints when we talk in prayer. Wanting us to express every detail that is important to us, a squinting God is totally unbound by the human constraints of time or energy or boredom! Made in the image of God, we humans have similar capacities to be good listeners if we exercise them.

᳘

VERSES FOR REFLECTION
"If anyone has ears to hear, let him hear. Consider carefully what you hear," he continued. "With the measure you use, it will be measured to you—and even more."
Mark 4:23-24

On the Wisdom of Not Burning Bridges

I ONCE READ OF A YOUNG MAN who no longer felt comfortable in the church he had been part of for seven years. The people were like family to him. Yet they didn't seem to share his interest in putting faith into practice, or even in discussing how faith applied to the current political situation of his country (England). By talking with the pastor before he left, he was able to transfer to a new church without burning bridges with the old.

If only everyone who broke off a long-term relationship used his good sense! But most of us are tempted to air all the dirty wash of the past when placed in the position of breaking ties.

One friend told me how crushed she was when a relative who had cared for her children for many years said she wouldn't continue. My friend felt angry and hurt.

Were her children misbehaving? Was she paying her relative too little?

But this woman decided not to burn any bridges, which wouldn't have worked very well anyway with a family member. Eventually, after a much-deserved break, the babysitter volunteered to care for the children again.

Sometimes we have to break relationships for one reason or another. We may feel called to leave a job, a church, or an organization where we've had long term involvement.

Sometimes people leaving jobs they didn't particularly like are tempted to tell off all the people they never had the nerve to level with. I remember hearing one man say he couldn't wait till he walked out of his factory on his last day, because then he was going to tell his supervisor exactly what he thought.

A young woman left a satisfactory job because she thought she had a better job at a new office. She departed with everyone's good wishes. But things didn't work out in the new job; she soon discovered she was in over her head. Then she ran into her former supervisor in a social setting and admitted things weren't working out too well. The supervisor said she could always come back.

Could she really? Since she hadn't burned bridges at her former place of employment, she was welcomed back with good-natured smiles. Because she had left with a good attitude, the door was open for her return.

In families where divorce has occurred, it's important that parents keep from burning bridges so both can continue to be parents. In such a close relationship, many feelings and experiences are mixed. The urge to hurt the other party can be almost overwhelming. But we all know who ends up getting hurt the most.

The comforting thing is that even when bridges *have*

been burned, they can be rebuilt (although with considerably more difficulty!) Conflict mediators, in particular, are skilled in helping neighbors, businesses and clients, employers and employees, and former spouses find solutions they can live with.

Jesus is the ultimate bridge-builder of course, making it possible for us to live as intimate members of God's family. Thank you, Jesus.

VERSES FOR REFLECTION

As a prisoner for the Lord, then, I urge you to live a life worthy of the calling you have received. Be completely humble and gentle; be patient, bearing with one another in love. Make every effort to keep the unity of the Spirit through the bond of peace.
Ephesians 4:1-3

Class Act

MY HUSBAND AND I were enjoying a modest evening without kids in a popular fast-food restaurant, when behind us we noticed an unusual flurry of activity.

Two college-age guys, in sharp suits and ties, breezed to a table with a large box. They whipped out a nice white tablecloth, good china for four, crystal, even candles and two roses. My curiosity—usually high about other people's business anyway—went off the Richter scale.

My privacy-minded husband tried at first to pretend nothing unusual was going on. Then he too had to smile and openly stare. Who were these guys and what were they trying to pull? Were they going to tape a commercial? Try to sell something? Commit a fraternity stunt?

Their preparation finished, they sat down and waited. And waited. Finally I just had to turn around and politely ask if they minded telling me what was going on.

"Well," they replied a little sheepishly, "we're supposed to meet two girls here, and we thought we'd surprise them."

Oh! Simple old romance. Old-fashioned courtliness

was still alive! How utterly sweet, I thought, and envied the lucky girls.

But the guys were still waiting. Eventually we could linger no longer, so we slowly and reluctantly prepared to leave. We just had to see the girls who would induce such a show of class.

As we pulled away, I could see the men were plainly concerned. It was now more than a half hour after their proposed meeting time. Poor guys: all gussied up—to make fools of themselves.

My envy turned to scorn. How could those girls do such a thing to such nice guys? Of course, I have no way of knowing the whole story. Maybe the guys were bores or notorious fast-movers. Maybe the women went to the wrong restaurant.

But what a good preparation for marriage, I thought! Just when you're expecting a big romantic evening, the kids get sick, the sitter can't come, or someone has to work late. Worse, sometimes in the flurry of going out, tempers flare and nobody's in the mood for the long-anticipated evening out.

But maybe it was a good reminder to me in another way as well. How often do I disappoint my long-suffering, patient spouse? When I tell jokes at his expense to appear funny in a crowd? When I give the gifts *I* want him to have, instead of what I know he really wants? When I just can't get around to mending his pants?

When I think of the things my husband has endured, college girls standing up two guys at Burgerland seems mild by comparison.

No spouse is perfect, but those of us whose spouses are loving, faithful, and supportive—and have never broken our hearts—need the grace to look past the little things that disappoint us.

I hope you'll find a way to let your spouse know the

things you appreciate about him or her, and a way to ask
forgiveness if you know you've been a disappointment.

➳

*Why do you look at the speck of sawdust in your brother's eye
and pay no attention to the plank in your own eye?*
Luke 6:41

To Couples Who Can't Decide

S HOULD WE, OR SHOULDN'T WE?" I remember deliberating as I watched other couples struggle with a screaming child in a supermarket. So often parents complain so much about the woes of potty training, sleepless nights, and messy mealtimes, that young couples may be scared off and decide not to bother with it all.

A newsmagazine article pointed out that so many of the very people equipped to raise intelligent, productive children are deciding not to have children or have only one. On the other hand, those caught in endless cycles of poverty with few opportunities often have larger families.

The decision to have or not have children is always a personal one: no one should tell anyone else what to do. I can think of a hundred and one things (at least) that would have been easier if we had not had children.

Still I'm thankful we were blessed with children. Here I offer my incomplete list of reasons to have children.

1. Children get you back in touch with your own childhood. How long has it been since you ventured down a turning, twisting slide? Adults look silly going down by themselves, but it's okay when you have a toddler on your lap.

2. Children get you back in touch with nature (if you ever got out of touch). Pausing with a three-year-old to listen to the birds makes you feel almost the same age yourself. I remember marveling that Doreen enjoyed touching the inchworms and earthworms which made me squeamish. Parents can find bottles for carrying ladybugs to school, get fresh aphids for them to eat, and carefully return the ladybugs to the garden after "show-and-tell."

3. Children help you remember how to laugh. I'm by nature quite serious. But even I couldn't help doubling over when I heard the children telling their own version of *The Three Bears* and noting that "Goldilocks laid down on the water bed."

4. Children, in many instances, help parents go back to church. And they help us see God. An out-of-the-blue question like "Mommy, how big is God?" suddenly lifts us from the dishpan to the celestial.

5. Children often seem to be the stimulus for a tremendous burst of creative and productive energy in their parents. Having *less* time to get things done, parents let unimportant things (like a perfect yard and house) take lower priority.

6. Children sometimes help their parents become more flexible—less addicted to their own lives and routines.

There are probably loftier and more profound reasons to have children; people often cite "someone to take care of me in my old age" and "a way to gain immortality" as reasons. But as someone has said, the only real reason to have children is because you *want* children in your life—not because of what they will grow up to be, or because of what they will give you in return.

≈§

Your children will be like olive shoots around your table.
Thus shall the man be blessed who fears the Lord.
Psalm 128:3b-4a (NRSV)

Kid Track

F LU AND STREP THROAT kept me home with the children for a day when the two youngest were six and three. They were sick but not too sick to want to play "office" with Mommy. Suddenly I found myself with *two* pint-sized bosses. One was far tougher and the other more lenient than any real-life bosses I've encountered.

Listen to these bosses, their comments preserved almost verbatim.

Six-year-old: "Now, I want an article finished for the paper *today*." (She hands me a paper and I decide to write down our conversation so she'll think I'm "writing.")

Me: "Today?"

"Yes, today. Start writing."

Three-year-old arrives with a play lunch of plastic food. "Ta da! Lunch!"

"Oh, lunch already?"

"Yes, I put ketchup and mustard on it."

"Oh, (chuckle) yes. I heard you going 'plop plop.'"

Six-year-old: "This is your lunch break."

I take two pretend bites.

Six-year-old: "Okay, start writing again."

"Hey! That was a short break!"

(Relenting.) "Well, you'll have another break later."

Three-year-old returns with a Big Mac box, hiding a smile. "Here's your break. You won't like it" (giggle).

I open the box. Instead of a hamburger, she has tucked in two treats like you get with a fast-food kid's meal.

"Oh, you gave me a Happy Meal!"

She grins her delight.

Six-year-old: "Now hand your paper to me when you're finished. I've drawn a picture to go with it . . ."

Once again I'm grateful to step inside my children's world, even if it takes a sick day to do it. What a luxury to sit and really play for several hours instead of trying to squeeze in quality time at the end of a hectic workday. It's always a revelation to hear kids playing back to us what they've caught from our work world.

Diehard career folks may scoff at my "mommy track." Women who mix motherhood with a career get side-lined on a mommy track rather than continuing on the fast track, proclaimed one book. My boss may raise an eyebrow when I have to stay home with sick kids, but it's a choice I want to make whenever possible.

There's no denying it. I am not advancing at the same rate as my colleagues in other offices. When I cannot travel at the whim of the company, when I cannot pursue further education because of relocating the whole family, when I drag my feet about overtime or evening meetings, I'm forced to admit I'm on the mommy track. While I'd like to call that the "parent track," I know only a few men (but there are some!) who stay home with sick kids, hold back on travel, and avoid relocating for the sake of their children.

So I can't have everything. Welcome to Real World 101, as they say.

I don't mean to point fingers at anyone for choices they make. I simply want to encourage us to make the most even of sick days. When we stay home with sick kids, it's tempting to sit them in front of the TV or VCR all day so we can continue business as usual. But I know from experience that trying to be truly present to sick children, in mind as well as body, rewards us with fresh feelings of family togetherness and love.

Of course, there's such a thing as too much of a good thing. Even the cheeriest parent gets weary when sickness stretches on for days at a time.

But why wait for a sick day to enter your child's world? Perhaps there's someone waiting, even now, for you to lay down the paper or turn off the TV. Getting on the "kid track" for an hour or two might bring you a few smiles and even a revelation or two! God is a parent too. Parenting helps us understand a little more fully God's love for us.

❧

VERSE FOR REFLECTION
But I have stilled and quieted my soul; like a weaned child with its mother, like a weaned child is my soul within me.
Psalm 131:2

Summer
Camp and the
Big Bad Wolf

D O YOU WANT ME TO get your jacket out for you?" I
asked, clucking over my seven-year-old in the process of saying good-bye before her first overnight camp.

Tanya shook her head.

She was only going to be gone two nights, but there I
was, fussing and stewing with a full-blown case of
"smotherhood."

"Can I take your picture?" I asked finally, "standing
here with the counselors?"

"No, Mom. *Bye.*"

"Are you sure you don't want your jacket?" I asked
again, fretting about how fast it had turned cool. The
counselor looked at me with a slight smile that seemed to
say, "Typical parent!"

Reluctantly we drove off then. When I turned I could

see Tanya still standing in the same place, looking around bravely and waiting for whatever lay ahead.

"We only packed one pair of long pants for her, like the brochure said," I worried on the way home. "I sure hope she doesn't get cold."

"And I wish they would have let us see around the camp," Stuart added.

I suppose sending your child to his or her first overnight camp is a rite of passage for parents and child alike. Not that all children want to go or get the opportunity. In fact, I was floored that Tanya even *wanted* to go to this beginner's camp since she, of all our children, throws the biggest fit when I go away.

The morning of departure she had her first sign of cold feet. After looking forward to it for weeks, she was quiet and withdrawn. Finally she softly told me, "I don't want to go to camp."

"That's natural," I assured her. "Everyone is worried about doing something for the first time." Beneath the Mr. Rogers calm, I panicked. *What if she* really *starts balking,* I thought. *We've already paid her fee.*

Then a tactic came to me. "Tanya, just think. When you come back you'll be able to tell Michelle [older sister] all about it and what *she'll* be doing next week when *she* goes." This seemed just the egging on she needed.

That night the other two girls chose as their bedtime story *The Three Little Pigs.* "Once upon a time Mother Pig decided it was time for her children to go out in the world and find homes for themselves," the fable begins. I was struck by the timing: we weren't just sending a child to camp, we were sending our child out into the world.

Perhaps parents make fools of themselves on the first day of camp, not just over clothes or an unfamiliar campground, but because we know all too well what may be ahead. Would there be wolves at camp for Tanya? Of course not real ones (although she spotted a deer on the drive to camp!). But would there be girls who were stuck-up, or boys who were mean? Would her counselor be more interested in guys than in the kids? Would Tanya eat anything for the two days? Would she whine about gnats and mosquitoes and make the counselors crazy?

I used to think Mother Pig was cold for pushing her piglets out on their own to a quick death. If you recall, the first piglet took the easy path toward town and bought straw for his home. It was easily blown away by the wolf.

The second pig took an "I'll wait and see" attitude and built a home of sticks. The third pig not only took on the difficult and tedious job of building a sturdy house of bricks but outwitted the wily wolf as well.

My question and, I have to think, the question the first teller of this story had in mind is, What kind of children am I raising? Will they take the easy way? Will they get blown away by the first wicked wolf that comes along?

Just when you worry you've done everything all wrong in parenting, your kids step out bravely to camp, to school, to college. Not knowing a soul, not having a clue what to expect—they cheerfully tell you, "Run along now." What a tribute to the grace of God!

Sometimes we feel safest in the nest, and God lets us know gently (or not so gently) that it's time to venture out. Can I bravely move out in faith, knowing that God, like an overprotective mother, will be right there?

෴

VERSES FOR REFLECTION

Are not five sparrows sold for two pennies? Yet not one of them is forgotten by God. Indeed, the very hairs of your head are all numbered. Don't be afraid; you are worth more than many sparrows.
Luke 12:6-7

Things Mother Didn't *Tell Me*

MOTHERS PREACH AT US from day one. Famous lines like "Eat your vegetables," "Wear your boots," and "Save your kisses for the one you marry," supposedly prepare us for each and every eventuality.

Then one day I realized there were a lot of wonderful things my mother *tried* to tell me—yet the advice fell on deaf ears until I became a mother myself. For instance, only recently did I realize how terrible I was to interrupt my mother's Sunday afternoon nap with an urgent question about the whereabouts of some shoes. My mother didn't say I was a selfish, thoughtless child. But her exhausted sigh and sharp "Find them yourself!" should have given me a hint.

On the flip side, Mother couldn't really tell me how euphoric it made her feel when we children straightened up the whole house for no reason at all. Just when insanity sets in, children offer you a spontaneous foot massage.

Mother couldn't really tell me why she broke down

and cried the Sunday morning there was a new baby in the house (fourth one) and a grandmother to comb and six little pigtails to braid.

Mother couldn't have told me how hard it was to worship God while feeling angry about the little bodies climbing over hers, begging for gum and snooping in her purse. Or how it made her heart leap to hear us posing lispy prayers to God and asking questions that showed we were learning in church even while fighting over chewing gum.

Mother didn't tell me that she felt like throwing us on the floor when we got her up for the fourth time in a single night. I never even *thought* about Mother wearily getting up in the night for *me* until I did it for my own (although I'd certainly heard about it).

Now I know just how unthinkable a mother's thoughts can become in the dark of night—and how brimming with love that same mother can be as she greets that rascal infant come the first light of day.

Mother didn't tell me how irritating it was to hear about glorious motherhood on Mother's Day from a male preacher who went to meetings seven nights a week. Or to be told, "Take time for your kids," when she was feeling, *Give me a break. I take time for these kids all day. I need time for myself!*

My mother didn't tell me some other things simply because society changes. She didn't tell me how lonely I would feel as I watched my preschoolers wave at me as I drove off to work. (Although she claims to have felt guilty about all the times she left us with Grandpa and Grandma when she left for volunteer work or church meetings, I have no memories at all of feeling cheated!)

Mother couldn't really tell me how badly she needed a night out with her husband. I remember, though, how carefully she sewed a new dress weeks in advance of such an event, and I remember her sparkle as she left the house on such nights.

I suspect that in the future I will find even more things my mother didn't prepare me for: the panic of waking and discovering that a child has not yet come home; the bittersweet tug of sending a child off to college; the specialness of having everyone home for a holiday.

Becoming a parent helps you appreciate and understand your own parents. (Of course, you can learn these things other ways as well; perhaps it's just a matter of growing up.)

But it helps me understand a little better, too, that the only way for God really to understand what it was like to be human was to become human in the person of Jesus on earth. Because Jesus was tempted and tried in every way we are, and because he suffered as much pain and abandonment as any human will ever suffer, we can know God truly understands how we feel.

The divine Parent would love to prepare us for every eventuality in life, but God lets us experience life fully ourselves. We can find comfort and encouragement in that knowledge, and it helps us understand God a little more fully.

෴

VERSES FOR REFLECTION

Therefore, since we have a great high priest who has gone through the heavens, Jesus the Son of God, let us hold firmly to the faith we profess. For we do not have a high priest who is unable to sympathize with our weaknesses, but we have one who has been tempted in every way, just as we are— yet was without sin.
Hebrews 4:14-15

Why Didn't I Just Raise Radishes?

W HEN THE CHILDREN WERE SMALL, they enjoyed a wonderful Sesame Street book featuring the tireless Cookie Monster. In it Cookie Monster frustrates a character so severely that this other character finally exclaims, in a nonsense kind of line, "Oh, why didn't I just raise radishes?"

It's a question I've asked myself many times when frustrated with parenting. However, there are countless other times I rejoice that I'm not just raising radishes but wonderful, God-created little human beings.

One time parents feel this way is when the kids come up with those cute, profound, or pithy sayings.

Big sister to younger sister: "Don't forget—a rule at our school is 'don't walk out of the bathroom with your pants still down!' "

Or the time I was pregnant with our third child. The four-year-old saw me reading a book. "Mommy, is that book about pregnancy?"

"No," I replied, "Why?"

"Well," she said, like a stern nurse, "you *should* be reading books about being pregnant."

It was at the beginning of this same pregnancy that I looked forward to sharing the news with three sisters, all of whom had been adopted. They were also used to having foster children in their family. When I excitedly shared the news that we were going to have a new baby, they smiled politely and one asked, "Do you mean *foster* or *adopted*?"

Kids are famous for their profundity in the religious department. I'm glad I wrote these down:

"Mommy, what comes *after* the New Testament?"

"If you say God doesn't need to sleep (Psalm 121—"God never slumbers"), why did Genesis say God rested?"

"Why don't they list the mothers?" (after hearing a genealogy from the Bible.)

"Did God write the Bible?"

My mom will never let me forget the time I asked her if, in her day, the Bible was written on scrolls.

One mother shared this gem after their church building burned to the ground. When the congregation gathered for singing at the charred site, one two-year-old admitted he "didn't feel like singing." A little later he had cheered up enough to suggest, "Well, maybe we could sing 'Building Up the Temple.' "

Kids never cease to be amazed at how old their parents are. One day, though, when I was complaining about being almost thirty-eight, the eight-year-old reminded me I was in my thirties, which really wasn't so far from being in my twenties.

Often kids like their own answers better than any you could supply. One evening six-year-old Tanya read a simple book to me all by herself. "Mommy, how did Mrs. Proctor teach me to read?"

"Well," I said, "it took a lot of practice and repeating, plus hard work."

"I think it's *magic*," Tanya explained.

Sometimes it's not so much a *saying* that prompts chuckles or a lump in the throat, but an action: a tissue brought for a crying sibling; a Cheerio shared with the family dog.

If we like to think of children coming to us fresh from the hand of God, I don't think it's too far-fetched to let their sayings—profound or embarrassing—speak to us and reach us in ways no adult could.

VERSES FOR REFLECTION

He called a little child and had him stand among them. And he said: "I tell you the truth, unless you change and become like little children, you will never enter the kingdom of heaven. Therefore, whoever humbles himself like this child is the greatest in the kingdom of heaven."
Matthew 18:2-4

Lessons from a Child-free Sister

I 'LL NEVER FORGET THE TIME my thirtysomething sister (nicknamed Pert) who was visiting us volunteered to rock the ten-month-old to sleep. Ten minutes passed, twenty. Was she having trouble getting Doreen to sleep, I wondered? Finally after thirty minutes, Pert emerged from the nursery, looking serene.

"Did you have a problem getting her to sleep?" I cautiously asked.

"Oh, I was just enjoying rocking my 'last' baby," she answered with a smile, referring to the fact that no more nieces or nephews were anticipated in our extended family.

How long had it been since I lingered while rocking a baby to sleep, relishing the intimacy of a sleeping child? Too often the moments I *did* manage to spend rocking were impatient: *Why won't she go to sleep?* I could be doing so many important things.

Although I don't recall her ever offering outright advice, my sister has unwittingly taught me many other lessons about parenting. A few summaries:

1. *It's okay to get tired of being a parent.* When Pert comes to visit for several days, she takes the children on walks, reads books until she's hoarse, and roughhouses on the floor. When she leaves she says happily, "Now I have my mothering instincts fulfilled for awhile." Strangely, I feel the same way sometimes—but can't drive off after a brief visit!

2. *Mothers aren't the only ones who are harried and work long hours.* As a college coach and athletic director, Pert often works until at least one in the morning. And she is gone almost every evening and many weekends. The next time a child wakes us up at 1:00 a.m. with an earache, I'll think of Pert and wonder if she's still up.

3. *I'm normal if I feel my blood pressure rising during morning rush hour.* One school morning when the children were small, my sister was visiting, I was getting ready for work, and the bus was due in fifteen minutes. Tanya needed help with her cereal, Doreen was waiting for a bottle, and the phone was ringing.

There sat the five-year-old, supposedly getting ready for school but actually fussing over an imaginary wrinkle in a sock. I thought Pert was still sleeping on the living room floor when I heard a low moan coming from her: "How can you *stand* to see her dawdling like that?"

4. *Parenting requires great physical stamina.* I've always been jealous of my sister's athletic prowess and outright strength. So I was unprepared for her reaction when she bathed our one-year-old in the bathtub and put her to bed one night. After finally getting her settled, my sister took a deep breath and asked, "How do you *ever* manage?" So *that's* why I feel like crawling in bed after the children are in!

5. *It's normal to want a break from kids sometimes.* Not all of the lessons are positive ones. Pert sometimes gets an overdose of the children. She may try to ignore a request for one more piggyback ride or be totally oblivious to the kids when they interrupt her while she's reading. Then I see myself, desperately trying to finish another chore instead of listening to the toddler at my heel.

6. The final lesson I'm learning is this: *I was a better aunt before I became a mother!* I too used to go on long walks, shop, bake cakes, and play in boxes with my nieces and nephews. Surely there's room in every family for the extra benefits of an aunt or uncle without children! They should be welcomed, not chided with "Well, when are you going to have some of your own?" or "But who will take care of you when you're old?" If they do a good job of "aunting" and "uncling," they'll probably have plenty of nieces and nephews who won't forget them when they get old.

Parents and children alike benefit from having other caring Christians influencing their children. Are there children who would welcome your love today?

◈

VERSES FOR REFLECTION

Each year his mother made him a little robe and took it to him when she went up with her husband to offer the annual sacrifice. Eli would bless Elkanah and his wife, saying, "May the Lord give you children by this woman to take the place of the one she prayed for and gave to the Lord."
1 Samuel 2:19-20

Bending the Rules

M Y FIVE-YEAR-OLD was heartbroken. We couldn't find the library book she had brought home from school and she wouldn't be allowed to bring another one home until she had returned that one. Sensible rule.

We hunted in all the logical places, then the illogical ones. My usual line about "I'm sure it will turn up" just didn't comfort her. On library day at school, she was always left out.

After three weeks of not getting anywhere, I called the school librarian and explained the situation. "I'll be glad to pay for the book," I offered, "so Tanya can start bringing books home again."

The librarian with the sensible rule also turned out to have a sensible head. "Well, books turn up so frequently soon after parents have paid for a book, I hate to go through all the book work," she said with the wisdom of years.

"I'll tell you what; since you called, I'll go ahead and let Tanya bring books home again. I know you'll be responsible. If you still haven't found it by the end of the year, then I'll let you pay."

I could have kissed her. Tanya's eyes, as she got off the bus that day, were my reward. "Mrs. Fisher let me have a book today!" she sang.

But I was still worried about the book. When I saw Mrs. Fisher several weeks later at school, I said we still hadn't found it. "You know," she said without a hint of condescension, "books so often turn up caught behind a bureau or desk right at the top of the baseboard. They don't slide down so you can see them from the floor, and it's hard to see behind the furniture."

I was sure I had looked in all those places, but I went home and checked behind older sister's platform bed. Sure enough, as though Mrs. Fisher had snooped through our house, there it was. That day Tanya's eyes really did shine when I showed her the lost book.

Somehow librarians have acquired a questionable reputation through the years of shushing little kids and frowning about overdue books. I'm glad the libraries my kids encounter aren't such places. Noise is frequent in the children's room, and overdue fines go to the library fund.

There are eye-catching displays and computers constantly in use and story times for toddlers. There are videos to check out and old-fashioned film strips the kids still love even in this day of video-everything. I've seen our public librarian believe a woman who said that she had never checked out the books in question, so she couldn't possibly owe the fine.

For my children, a trip to the library ranks right up there with a trip to the park. Allowing children to read for pleasure and to choose the books they want (instead of assigning their reading) can help them develop a life-long interest in reading.

So I'm thankful for the librarian who made a big difference by influencing my daughter even before she began to read. Now instead of fearing the big librarian with the authority to make the rules, I'm sure my daughter feels fondness.

There is place for rules and regulations to keep our public and school libraries solvent, functioning places. But blessed be all librarians who know when and how to bend a rule.

Do I know when and how to bend the rules at times, and when I need to stick to my guns? God, give me the wisdom of this librarian!

ᴥᴥ

VERSES FOR REFLECTION

I have not stopped giving thanks for you, remembering you
in my prayers. I keep asking that the God of our
Lord Jesus Christ, the glorious Father,
may give you the Spirit of wisdom
and revelation, so that you
may know him better.
Ephesians 1:16-17

When the Kids Grow Up

W E ALL KNOW THAT CHILDHOOD is characterized by frequent sighs of "When *I* grow up," heard with increasing anxiety as the kids get older.

Now I know that parents have frequent sighs of their own, mostly starting with "when the kids grow up."

I was trying to find the front of my refrigerator the other day when I decided that when my kids are grown, the front of my refrigerator will be so clean I'll see myself on it. Furthermore, I won't keep a single drawing or memo there. I won't even own a refrigerator magnet.

When my kids are grown, I'll go to the mall without making three emergency trips to the bathroom.

When the kids are grown, you won't see shoes permanently planted in my living room.

I'll drive right by McDonalds and eat something nice and Chinese.

I'll go to the doctor's office and read grown-up magazines instead of *The Cat in the Hat.*

I'll walk by the most dreaded place in the grocery store and not buy any gum or mints.

I'll sit down to breakfast without people fighting over who gets the prize in the cereal box.

I'll go to the mall without going to the toy store.

I'll take a nice hot bath without removing forty-two bath toys first.

I'll leave on a business trip without worrying that the school will call and say that one of the kids is sick.

I'll wake up on a Saturday morning and bake bread, sew a skirt, or take a hike in the woods at my whim.

When the kids grow up, my husband will finish a complete sentence—maybe even a whole conversation with me—without interruption.

We'll go out to eat and get by for a small sum instead of a ransom.

I'll sit through worship services without shushing anybody or passing out pencils, gum, and offering money.

Oh, I'll suffer occasional pangs of nostalgia for all of the above—but mostly I'll miss these things as much as I now miss changing diapers in the middle of the night.

I think.

Of course, I thought growing up to be a wife and a mother and have a career would be infinitely better than having to study and be bossed around and live on an allowance.

Isn't it funny how often we find ourselves waiting and longing for the next stage?

I was reminded of that recently when good friends had their first child, and I found myself staring at the baby longingly through the hospital window. I envied the parents as I thought of giving the baby her first bath, feeding her, holding such a hunched up little ball of humanity.

Then I had to remember that when *I* was a new mother, I envied parents whose children were already out of diapers, going to school, or at least independent enough that you could cook a meal without having a toddler clinging to your legs.

I do know this: I *will* miss all of the ways my children have put me in touch with God, with laughter, with play, with enjoying bright autumn walks.

This is called dealing with life's continuing passages, and people have written whole books about it! Most of the time I'm too impatient with the present, always dreaming about things to come.

Maybe an empty refrigerator door will look kind of . . . lonely. What do you think?

VERSES FOR REFLECTION

*There is a time for everything, and a season for every activity
under heaven: a time to be born and a time to die,
a time to plant and a time to uproot.*
Ecclesiastes 3:1-2

How to Really Enjoy Your Vacation

I DON'T THINK I'VE ever regretted a dollar I've spent on travel.

I've been sorry about buying certain clothes. I've gnashed my teeth over wrong furniture choices and poorly chosen toys. I've regretted certain brands of foods and cars themselves—but never where they take me.

To be sure, there have been plenty of "How did I get myself into this?" moments when tempers flared and blame flowed freely.

I remember sweat rolling off us in the middle of the California desert and a flat tire on a busy Louisiana freeway. I remember riding all the way to Florida from Virginia squashed with three others in a back seat. There was the night I slept in Paris' Orly Airport because my girlfriends and I were too cheap to get a hotel room. And

I remember eating orange-pineapple ice cream for breakfast in an Ontario motel because it was left over from the night before and we had to use it up.

Since I love to travel, I have to ask myself, Why am I such a gadabout?

I probably inherited it from my parents. If they lacked money for a trip, they could always take a few choice pigs from the barn and get some easy money. Only now that I'm grown can I appreciate the luxury our parents gave us through the gift of frequent travel.

People who don't enjoy traveling much or place little priority on it can always think of a million things they'd rather spend their money on. "What do you *have* after a trip? I'd rather spend money on a new couch we can enjoy for ten years."

Travel can give you memories that will outlast even the sturdiest sofa. There is something deeply satisfying about seeing on TV a place you've visited and saying, "I was there!"—Travel can enhance relationships—either with your traveling companions (despite testy moments) or with people you visit en route. At times we're lucky enough to discover a quaint restaurant; some unspoiled natural beauty; or even an interest in geography, history, or bird watching.

But then maybe it's just the *idea* of travel I love so much. I love the anticipation, planning, buying new things for a trip. I don't even mind packing; everything is organized in the beginning. I love the smell of a fresh airline ticket and especially love getting up early when there's a little fog and the morning has that special June atmosphere we kids used to call a "trip morning." And I also love reminiscing and getting photos back from the developer and hauling out souvenirs.

But do I *really* like sitting three hours in one position with a full bladder and growling stomach and no exit for twenty miles? Do I really like crawling ten miles per hour through a tunnel with one lane closed as kids howl in the back seat? Do I really like hunting for the toddler's shoes in the mess that was once so neat when we roll into a rest stop? And do I really like waking up in the car at 2:00 a.m. when Stuart has pulled over, saying, "Okay, *you* can drive now."

Perhaps travel is a metaphor for life in that so much of life we spend anticipating events, vacations, next phases of development, tomorrow, next week, next year. We also love looking back on the good times. But how often do we enjoy the present as we live it, "every, every minute," as Thornton Wilder wrote?

Travel doesn't bring true happiness. If you can't travel or vacation as much as you'd like, concentrate on enjoying whatever moments of free time you have. Put aside thoughts of next year. Focus on the good traits of the people around you. Put aside past regrets and failures. Tell yourself, "It doesn't get any better than this. This is life. This is now." And thank God for life in all its fullness *and* everyday-ness.

ܐܶ

VERSES FOR REFLECTION
The Lord is my shepherd, I shall lack nothing.
He makes me lie down in green pastures,
he leads me beside quiet waters.
Psalm 23:1-2

Who Does the Dirty Work?

O NE DAY I ACCIDENTALLY cut the palm of my hand when a choke lever on the lawn mower broke off. It was not a big deal, but the cut took several weeks to heal.

What surprised me was the number of times I went to use that part of my palm—the base of the thumb—and couldn't because it was too painful to push against. For instance, slamming the trunk of a car was difficult.

Why is it that we never realize one body part's usefulness until we lose use of it for awhile? Overlooked, unappreciated, taken for granted, our palms rate right down there with feet in terms of unappreciated function.

Like a lowly foot or palm, janitorial work has to be one of the most overlooked, underappreciated parts of an organization. No one notices your work unless you *don't* shine the faucets. I became aware of this when our church janitor was gone for several weeks. Persons from the church were asked to fill in. Somehow service takes on new meaning when you're down on hands and knees cleaning up someone else's spills.

But being a janitor or a cleaning woman is difficult in more ways than an occasional distasteful job. It is difficult because in our society being a janitor is not a high status job. Too many people *look down* on the janitor. This is strange, because "clean" is something most people value highly. The first requirement for a restaurant—even above good food—is cleanliness.

I'd guess that at school clean children, on average, get more respect and affection than dirty ones. Tips for job hunting always include, "Be neat and clean. Look your best." In hospitals, cleanliness is literally a matter of life and death; for that reason cleaning personnel are sometimes given a little more status. At least when I talked to one housekeeper, she said she felt her job was really important to the overall functioning of the hospital.

I'm not suggesting applying fancy titles like "sanitation associate" to janitors. I'm talking basic human respect here. So often we treat janitors as if they were furniture. Out of practice and long tradition, a cleaning woman keeps her eyes averted when passing others in a hall.

We can begin to look at persons who clean for a living in a new light. That can happen by striking up a simple conversation; ask how busy she feels, ask about family news, discuss the weather—as you'd do with any other work associate. It can happen by thinking about the many acts of cleaning most of us do in a day's time. There is nothing degrading about washing the car, cleaning our homes, brushing our teeth. So why do we look down—even for a moment—at someone who works full-time at cleaning? The title of this meditation is probably even a misnomer because, as someone commented, it's only "dirty" work if you view it that way.

I cleaned houses one summer. At one house, I felt like

a maid allowed to fix my own drinks, but the woman would disappear to a full calendar of social events while I worked.

At the other house, I felt like the woman's *friend* coming in to help out. On days she had big jobs for me to do like windows or cupboards, she *helped* me to make the job go faster. She always asked about my family, and she often fixed coffee or a soda for me.

The jobs were the same, but my feelings about them were different because each boss had a different way of relating to me.

I'd guess that many people who clean for a living enjoy their work. Your mind can do many things while you sweep, dust, and scrub. You can leave your work at the office and sometimes have a flexible schedule.

But I'd also guess there isn't a cleaning person alive who at some point hasn't felt like an unappreciated palm or foot, not noticed until something goes wrong.

The same underappreciation happens in families and churches, no matter what kind of job we're talking about. You don't have to be the janitor to feel taken for granted. Paul wrote the wonderful passage in 1 Corinthians 12 for just such a reason—showing us that the feeling is hardly anything new! The next chapter gives the remedy that helps people feel appreciated: love.

❧

VERSES FOR REFLECTION

There are different kinds of gifts, but the same Spirit. There are different kinds of service, but the same Lord. There are different kinds of working, but the same God works all of them in all [people].
1 Corinthians 12:4-6

Chicken House Therapy

WHILE CANNING AND PRESERVING fruits and vegetables is in one sense a joy (I love to hear the telltale "ping" of a jar sealing!), I'm glad we don't have gardens and harvest all year long.

But it was while I was snapping beans one day that I was struck again by the wonderful way the mind is free to roam when hands are busy in routine, automatic work. The children were occupied with a visiting cousin. Although I could have asked them to help, somehow I just enjoyed the hour or so alone, hands flying, being productive, mind flying just as fast.

I wasn't thinking about anything specific. My mind wandered to our church, to my job, to thinking of relationships with the children, to what I wanted to be doing in ten years and how I might accomplish that.

It was the kind of thinking I haven't had much time for since the days my best thinking occurred (this may be stretching it) in the chicken coop.

Oh, it was a pretty fancy chicken coop, to be sure, especially in those days. The coop had hens in cages and long cement aisles over which an egg gatherer pushed carts, picking up dozen after dozen of clean, perfect eggs. Hen droppings rarely spoiled the reverie. If anything functioned as therapy for me during those growing-up years, it was those chickens. They were a captive audience, cocking their heads this way and that as I talked out my problems. I sometimes ranted, sometimes cried in frustration or joy, and sometimes warbled at the top of my lungs.

Mind you, only in retrospect can I talk so longingly about my chicken house therapy. How we hated to gather eggs back then! How Mother must have hated shooing us to the chicken house twice a day: "Come on, go gather eggs," she'd remind us. "You have to be done in time to eat." We were paid a small amount which helped motivate us.

But besides teaching us the value of work and a dollar earned, I now realize how manual, repetitive work contributed to my having time and space to think things out.

What makes me be able to sing the praises of repetitive labor is not having to do it at my paid job. For people who sit all day—meeting, dictating, thinking, writing, or planning—repetitive work during off time lets the brain rest. Another kind of thinking can emerge, the freewheeling, daydreaming, one-thought-leads-to-another kind of thinking.

For people who do repetitive work in a factory or elsewhere, just changing locations and type of work at the end of the day can be a relief. If there is energy left, the mind may enjoy sewing a new dress or tinkering with a car engine. Finding balance and a change of pace can be a key to enjoying both leisure and paid time.

You might want to keep that in mind in choosing volunteer work and entertainment. If you sit all day and answer telephones, you probably won't want to help out with fundraiser phoning; pitching in to assemble hoagie or sub sandwiches would bring more relief. One woman who works with money told me she's always asked to be the treasurer of any club she's in. She's learned to turn that job down for her own sanity.

Jesus was a carpenter by occupation. We often say Jesus didn't begin his active ministry until he was thirty years old. But maybe Jesus began to ruminate on the outline for his beloved Sermon on the Mount there in the carpenter shop while sanding wood.

Use your "mindless" work—whatever it is—to balance the other parts of your life! You can meditate, pray, hum, or whistle. Use the time to walk more closely with God.

✥

VERSE FOR REFLECTION

Oh, how I love your law! I meditate on it all day long.
Psalm 119: 97

Advice from a Blue-Collar Man

A SCHOOL BOY WAS TOURING a factory and the plant guide was explaining how the little handheld computer and wand kept track of inventory. The seventh grader commented to the worker, "Boy, you've got it made!"

Fancy technology may have made some work easier for factory workers (and in some cases made it more complicated), but the truth is that hardly anyone wants to end up working in a factory. Yet where would we be without factory workers?

I once heard someone say that in North America we stand on the shoulders of the working class—yet take that so much for granted. Our system of life as we know it—the cheap clothes; convenient food; factory-built cars, homes, and furniture—would fall apart without the millions of people who punch clocks and do basically one thing all day.

At one level, factory workers today have benefits and

protection that their counterparts in past eras didn't have. Sometimes they even make good money. But often even a fairly good job in a decent factory plus working overtime still puts you near the poverty line.

My husband is a factory worker. I think my husband would tell that schoolboy to stay in school and "do good" so he could do so simple a thing as take off work to get dental work done without having his attendance record flawed (Stuart usually uses a day of vacation). I don't know how factory workers are supposed to go to the doctor or dentist. Finally, a few professionals have realized there is a huge market of people who would appreciate evening hours.

And family needs? If the children are sick, need doctor appointments, or stay home because of snow, the spouse gets stuck with all those details. In families where there are two blue-collar workers, emergencies are even tougher to handle.

The real rub comes because many people hold deep-seated prejudices toward such workers and don't even know it. One doesn't need to be a different color to feel stared at in most churches or upscale places of business. Just walk in wearing a polyester dress from the '70s and an older style of shoes and feel the noses go up. Or open your mouth in a Sunday school to express a few opinions you didn't get in college and you'll hear feet shuffling.

I've noticed this type of snootiness when I stop in a store on my lunch hour while dressed for the office. No problem. I'm treated promptly (usually) and with courtesy.

It's different when I dash to town on my days off with three kids in their play clothes whose hair I haven't had time to comb. Salespeople look like they think, "Oh, here's just a mother with three kids who doesn't have much money."

Maybe I'm just imagining it. I'd like to *believe* that, but then sometimes I'm guilty of such snootiness myself. We are all prone to snap judgments, whether we write off a well-dressed businessman as stuck up, or whether we look down on a woman wearing hot-pink pants and a tight shirt. One woman told me about a well-to-do Christian businessman who felt he had to underdress to be accepted at church.

In most circles, discrimination on the basis of class is as real as discrimination on the basis of color. The job, educational achievements, financial status, and the social circles we move in determine how we are treated. Can we ever get to the place where we can truly evaluate people by only one criterion: Is this a human being? Then he or she is loved by God and so I must treat him or her that way.

Isn't that, after all, the way you like to be treated?

≈§

VERSES FOR REFLECTION
*I ask you, therefore, not to be discouraged because of my
sufferings for you, which are your glory. For this
reason I kneel before the Father.*
Ephesians 3:13-14

A Limited *Praise* *of Busyness*

O NE EVENING MY HUSBAND and I were trying to accomplish a half dozen things at once. A storm had knocked down several large limbs off our maple trees. I needed to run a new book manuscript off my computer printer. And I had to wash a load of clothes.

I set up the computer to print, got the clothes started, then went out to prop limbs so Stuart could saw them up.

"Do you realize that 100 years ago our grandparents would have considered this science fiction?" I mused during a break from the chain saw. "They would have been out here using an ax on the tree. They would have written a book with paper and pencil. And they would have washed with a scrubboard. But they never could have had all three going on simultaneously!"

"So how come we still feel like we never get anything accomplished?" Stuart contemplated.

Indeed! Someone has pointed out that even with our

modern washers and dryers, North Americans may still spend more hours a week on laundry than their South American counterparts who wash by hand in a stream. We simply have so many more clothes.

After waxing the floor late one Saturday night, I decided to call my parents who live in a different time zone. It had been a particularly exhausting weekend, with a wedding, cleaning up for company, and a school musical.

"So how are you?" I asked Mom and Dad.

"Exhausted—I'm looking forward to Sunday," came Mom's reply.

"And I thought I was looking forward to retirement!" I responded.

Many of the sixty-five-year-olds I know seem as busy as my thirty- to forty-year-old friends. I was at a business lunch one day when the only person to come late and leave early, because of other obligations, was officially retired. What are these retirees doing wrong?

But when pushed, most of us wouldn't have it any other way. Mom frequently gets bored and lonely on too-quiet Sundays. If we have a weekend with nothing planned, I invent work by inviting company. We get ourselves off one committee only to be enticed into a new project. Maybe we need to stop chiding ourselves for being too busy and recognize that human beings are happiest when involved in meaningful, productive activity.

Now I will be the first to raise a caution about overwork, addiction to work, and keeping priorities straight. I will be first to sing the praises of a quiet evening at home and the need to find time for feeding the inner spirit. When headaches pound, ulcers churn, or back muscles tighten, these signal too much of a good thing. There are times when busyness makes me lose control of my emotions and I scream at my kids or cry in the bedroom.

We spend a lot of time putting down the Protestant

work ethic most of us were raised on: "Idleness is the devil's workshop." "He who doesn't work doesn't eat." Maybe I'm a hopeless workaholic because of the way I was raised—but for the most part I'm happiest when I have a manageable workload.

Even kids seem happier when they have appropriate, kid-sized chores. My children complain about Saturday morning cleanup, but if I break the work down into a list of jobs they can check off as they finish, they seem to prefer something to do over being bored. I frequently catch one daughter humming as she works.

But it *is* hard to teach children the importance of learning to work when it is so much easier to do it ourselves. I keep reminding myself it is just as important that they learn to work as it is that they learn to read.

What children—and all of us—need is permission to take a break, to change the routine. I love and look forward to vacations, to weekends, and to nine o'clock when the kids are in bed.

Meaningful work and busyness are enjoyed the most when we also experience the opposite: meaningful breaks and periods of rest. Perhaps that is the real message of Genesis 2:2 (below) and the Old Testament teaching about sabbaticals. If God needed rest, how much more do we?

◄§

VERSES FOR REFLECTION

By the seventh day God had finished the work he had been doing; so on the seventh day he rested from all his work. And God blessed the seventh day and made it holy, because on it he rested from all the work of creating that he had done.
Genesis 2:2-3

How to Make a Committee Work

GOT AN IDEA?
Appoint a committee!
Watch nothing happen.
Why?

It's not only that committees are terrific dullers of anything creative. (Which is ironic, because committees are not this way on purpose. But committees are frequently made up of good creative people who all have ideas of their own and can't resist improving, critiquing, and brainstorming new angles. And so the original idea gets watered down, changed to an unrecognizable form, or simply lost.)

Committees frequently don't work because when someone *is* assigned to put an idea into action, he meets roadblocks in trying to carry out the assignment. If budget isn't a problem, then lack of personnel or volunteers to work on the idea is.

The implementer runs into someone who doesn't like the idea, who thinks of a different angle, or who requests that the job be handled in a different way. The implementer can't explain the lovely rationale the committee came up with, and the boss is sure it won't work.

So it's back to the committee with the idea for further discussion. But the committee can't meet for a month because Joe, Sue, and David are out of town and Jill is only available Thursdays. Ever wonder why it takes so long for committees to get anything done?

If I sound disillusioned by committee work, don't be fooled. I love to sit in committees. I love to sit around brainstorming, dreaming, arguing, thinking. It's the easiest work there is (although I won't deny you can get dead tired from sitting in meetings all day). It's putting ideas into action that gives me greater difficulty. People chosen for committees are often great "idea" people who have trouble delegating work to others and communicating great ideas to others; or they just don't have the people contacts or skills to get the idea off the ground.

Ideas need people to make them a reality—people to supply elbow grease and money; to make phone calls in the middle of helping kids with homework, making supper, and letting the dog out; to research names and addresses, unearth obscure facts, go to stores and find products or the best prices; to call caterers and retreat centers; to plan menus and figure out how to keep hot food hot and cold food cold; to remember the coffee stirrers or an adaptor plug for the VCR. Ideas need the detail people who count it their highest priority in life to cross things off their lists as fast as they can.

I know such people. They rarely accept committee assignments, because they've been frustrated by such processes. Too often wonderful ideas are dreamed up in highbrow committees without regard to whether it will actually work on the "assembly line."

I once read that if no one is willing to work on a project, if you can't get volunteers—then that activity probably is not important enough to do. We might get rid of some of our busyness if we would learn that simple truth: "If no one wants to do an activity or project, don't do it." Bake sales might not be held, organizations would go unfunded, organizations would die. And we'd all gain one more evening a week at home. Revolutionary!

Of course, maybe I'm oversimplifying, because organizations that have bake sales or send children door-to-door selling things accomplish good, worthwhile, life-changing things. And there is also the problem that in any group there are bound to be overlooked or underused people.

There's got to be another way! What we need instead of committees are "do-it-ees"—groups of people committed, up front, to *accomplishing* a task. These people should be those who get a thrill, not from coming up with the best idea, but from seeing an idea put to work.

I wonder what God thinks of our proliferation of committees, task forces, boards. I'm glad seeing God in our everyday walks is not a matter left up to a committee but an area where we can "just do it."

∾§

VERSES FOR REFLECTION

Your statues are my heritage forever; they are the joy
of my heart. My heart is set on keeping your
decrees to the very end.
Psalm 119:111-112

Invite a Friend

T HERE WAS A SMALL SIGN close to a shopping center that I probably passed at least once and up to three times a week. Depending on how long it had been there, I'd probably seen the sign hundreds of times. But I never really noticed it until one ordinary day. All the sign had on it was the name of a car battery brand.

Why would I suddenly become aware of a sign for batteries?

I had just come back from a convention in Nashville, Tennessee, where another convention at the same hotel was for people who work for this same battery company. Not being mechanically literate, I had never even heard of the brand before (my husband later informed me it is well known). But here I was meeting all these nice battery people in elevators, bathrooms, restaurants, and shops.

Now this is not about batteries or conventions or even my mechanical stupidity. It is rather about why I finally *noticed* a sign I must have seen hundreds of times before.

Has this happened to you? You learn a new word; in a couple days you see or read it three or four times. Your water heater goes bad and suddenly the newspaper is full of ads for water heaters just in time to solve your problem. The point is that the mind generally notices only what it has firsthand or personal experience with.

Maybe this is why much church advertising seems ineffective. You may have noticed an increase in the amount and creativity of church ads in recent years, from Episcopal to Lutheran to Mennonite to Presbyterian.

The "Episcopal" ads (not officially launched by the Episcopal headquarters) have won awards and attracted much attention in the press and church. Catchy, humorous, and sometimes-too-cute headlines like "Now that your kids can name the nine reindeer, shouldn't they be able to name the twelve apostles?" stand out from the ordinary. Yet many mainline Protestant churches continue their downward numerical slide.

It's the old "battery" problem. Most of us don't pay attention to or have any interest in a specific church until we can connect it with a *person*. All kinds of statistics show that most persons begin attending a church through the invitation of a *friend*. It's the personal connection that counts.

I'd guess that if you had an in depth conversation with an Episcopal co-worker on Friday, any ad for that particular church would jump out at you for the next few weeks. Otherwise the ad would just vanish into the usual advertising clutter.

Many of us are shy about inviting others to church. We've seen so many people turned off. We don't want to embarrass ourselves or our friends. We're quicker to tell others about the new restaurant we've discovered than to sing the praises of the church we've gone to for ten years.

Will I ever actually *buy* the brand of battery I'll always

connect with that Nashville convention? I don't know. I do know this: I wouldn't ever buy one without knowing about one. And then I probably wouldn't buy one without the personal invitation or recommendation of someone I trust.

So how come we expect people to enter our church just because it's sitting there in the middle of the block? How come it's so hard for me to tell others about the satisfaction and fulfillment I find in being a Christian? Why is it that many of us don't invite friends to church? How can we help others find God, if we really love God?

VERSES FOR REFLECTION

Therefore go and make disciples of all nations, baptizing them in the name of the Father and of the Son and of the Holy Spirit, and teaching them to obey everything I have commanded you. And surely I am with you always, to the very end of the age.
Matthew 28:19-20

Why Doesn't God Come Down?

I HAD TO DASH OUT during the middle of a day-long seminar on the future shape of Christian education to shuttle some nursery schoolers home.

"I don't believe in Santa Claus," Brian chattered (a few weeks before Christmas). " 'Cause how could he come down a chimney?"

I had not come up with a response by the time his busy, wonderful mind had linked this problem with another.

Pausing, he looked at me with the biggest black eyes. "Why doesn't *God* come down?"

"You mean to earth?"

"Yeah."

"You mean why can't we see God?"

Brian solemnly nodded.

In that instant all the theorizing I had heard that morning about the shape of Christian education and the future came alive. Here was a teaching moment more valuable than the best planned Sunday school lesson. Here was a bright four-year-old asking the question of the ages, a question theologians and philosophers have pondered and debated.

We were already at his stop. I put the van in park and gave him a big smile. "That's a wonderful question, Brian, one that lots of people think about."

Then I tried to put into brief, simple words the idea that God *did* come "down" to earth in the form of baby Jesus. But Jesus had to go back to live with God. Now we can't see Jesus or God anymore except in the loving, sharing things people do for each other.

That was still a bit hard for anyone, whether four or forty, to understand. But Brian's face changed from quizzical to satisfied-for-now, and he hopped out of the van.

As I drove away, marveling at the ability of children to cut through verbiage and double-talk, I had to think about the larger question behind Brian's stated one. Why doesn't God come down as people suffer, nations go to war, and natural disasters take their toll? How can a loving God sit back and allow all the terrible stuff to go on?

I find comfort in acknowledging that much of the terrible stuff is caused by people. Wars, illness, accidents, and crime happen because people make mistakes, miscommunicate, don't pay attention to warnings about drinking or smoking—on and on. And natural disasters are just that: disasters caused by forces in nature. I don't believe God sits around pulling strings on hurricanes to make them hit one town and avoid the next.

So is God powerless to intervene in the affairs we humans engage in or to change the course of a disaster or accident? No. But just as God gave Adam and Eve the gift of free choice and they chose to disobey, ultimately bringing disaster on themselves and all of us, so we have the gift of choice. Even if we find ourselves suffering all the calamities that came to a person like Job in the Old Testament, we still have the choice to persevere in spite of suffering or to succumb to it. That puts God in the role of Comforter and Strength-giver.

In the Old Testament, much of the language about God does cast God in the role of revenge-taker, sending plagues and destruction on those who don't follow God's way. Such thinking is also present in the New Testament—for instance, in the story of the man born blind.

The disciples asked Jesus, "Who sinned, this man or his parents, that he was born blind?" (John 9:2). Neither he nor his parents, said Jesus. The man was blind "so that God's power might be seen at work in him" (9:3, TEV).

This might be a hard answer to accept when we're suffering. But Christians who have lived through tragedy often see the power of God at work even in suffering.

When we ask, "Where is God amid suffering?" we can know that God (whether or not we admit or recognize it) can be there giving us strength to go on. Someone put it this way: "I think God's heart breaks with ours in tragedy, and God puts loving arms around us as we grieve."

All of this becomes more real as the loving actions of friends, family, and church help us in concrete ways. A meal brought in, coffee shared, a card, transportation, clothes, a squeeze on the arm. Then God truly does come down!

❧

VERSE FOR REFLECTION

As a mother comforts her child, so will I comfort you; and you will be comforted over Jerusalem.
Isaiah 66:13

Double Dare

F OR A LONG TIME I was uncomfortable about an incident
that happened as we were traveling peacefully down
the interstate one day. We were coming home from an
idyllic Sunday afternoon visit to a nearby city park. Suddenly the car in front of us pulled sharply onto the shoulder. The driver flung his door open wide and jumped
down on the pavement in an apparent rage. I could see
there was also a passenger.

The driver reached into the car, pulled out something
and threw it on the blacktop. There was a puff of smoke.
Then I could no longer see anything in the rearview mir-
ror.

You may not feel it's fair to leave the story hanging
there, but that is all I could see or was ever able to find
out. I assume it was nothing too serious or we would
have read about it in the paper.

But I wondered whether we should we have done
something. If so, what? How much risk is reasonable
when you have three small children in the car?

That leads me to a larger, everyday question: in a

world crying out with need, what can I do? I hide behind the excuse of "with three small children and a mortgage," what can I do to make the world a better place?

Then our pastor dares us to do "something crazy," to stick our necks beyond where we're normally comfortable, reminding us that Jesus was considered crazy by his contemporaries and even his family. Mark 3:21 says "When his family heard about this, they went to take charge of him, for they said, 'He is out of his mind.' "

Then I read a disturbing story about the children of peace warriors Philip Berrigan and Elizabeth McAlister. Together Philip and Elizabeth have spent five crucial years away from their children—in prison—for acts of civil disobedience carried out because of their convictions.

I personally do not carry my peace convictions to the point of civil disobedience, but I'm touched by those who feel a call from God to put their comfort and even their lives on the line. They are prophets in the tradition of the Ezekiels and Jeremiahs in the Old Testament, so burdened by a cause that they feel that a faith response to God involves nothing less than committing their whole lives to bearing the message.

What is a faithful response? When is it faithful to stay home, raise my children to the best of my ability, and hope they'll be the ones to make the world a better place? When is that an excuse, because they can use the same line of reasoning when they grow up?

Perhaps the answer lies somewhere between both extremes. There is something to be said for raising the next generation to the best of our abilities (which requires, time, commitment, and presence). But most of us have time to commit to other causes along the way as well.

Maybe my current situation means I won't go to work in a refugee camp at present. But could we invite a Fresh

Air child to spend time with our family? Could I find a way to help, with the children, at our church's clothing distribution center? Could we take flowers, bread, or a fresh pie to the new neighbors? Could I encourage my children to invite their friends to church or summer Bible school? Could we visit a nursing home on a regular basis? There are ways of doing helpful things that don't have to exclude children, though it's not easy or convenient to do even these simple deeds.

The bonus is that children, in seeing their parents pay more than lip service to helping others, are raised in the best way possible to in turn make the world a better place when they grow up.

The "double" in my title is not just a childish taunt, but a nudge to parents (myself included) to find ways to take responsible risks to serve others. We can look for activities and projects that include *both* children and parents. Can I take the dare?

❧

VERSE FOR REFLECTION

In the same way, any of you who does not give up everything he has cannot be my disciple.
Luke 14:33

Simplify, Simplify!

T HE FIRST TIME I HEARD the term *endowed chair*, I thought it was a euphemism for a wide-seated person. When my alma mater started having such things (endowed chairs, that is) I decided it was time to find out what the term meant. Just another way, it turned out, of collecting money for a specific department at the college.

This is an example of how we sometimes make simple things complex. (Of course, one could argue that "endowed chair" is simpler than "fundraising for the education department.")

Here's another instance. The owner of a radio station in southern Arkansas told this story on herself recently. They don't get much snow at that end of Arkansas, so when they got a big one in 1987 (I think it was), everyone was calling the radio station asking, "How deep is the snow?" No one at the station knew how to measure it. Surely one needed a fancy instrument.

So they called the U.S. Weather Bureau and said, "We've got a crazy question down here: How do you measure snow?"

Came the reply, "Well we've got a crazy answer for you. Get yourself a yardstick, push it down in the snow, and when you hit bottom, you read the yardstick."

They had twelve inches.

We're masters at making the simple complex. I had always put the twelve disciples of the Bible on a pedestal for so quickly leaving all to follow Jesus. What charisma Christ must have had, I reasoned. What commitment the disciples showed!

Then a guest minister at our church started her sermon one Sunday by saying, in reference to the calling of the disciples, "As a wife and mother, I don't see what's so wonderful about a bunch of men who go off on a fishing trip one morning and don't come home for three years. If someone were to offer *me* a three-year sabbatical with no dishes or clothes to wash, no responsibilities of any kind; to go off and wander around the country with a wonderful teacher, listening to stories and learning great truths, you wouldn't have to ask *me* twice!" So the disciples' commitment may not have been so lofty and complicated as I was making it!

"Simplify, simplify," said Henry David Thoreau. "Our life is frittered away by detail."

How I believe that! One summer when my husband was working night shift, I decided to write down all of the little things I did from the minute I got home from work (and he left for work) until I got into bed. I'll spare you the details, but talk about a list an arm long—mine literally was. My list didn't include big things, but stuff like checking out the pink thing Tanya found in the tree "that may be important, it may be poisonous" (it was an old cherry seed), getting food out of the freezer, putting clothes in the dryer, watering the flowers, changing diarrhea diapers, mowing a missed patch of lawn, putting straw around the onions. The list also included the notation that we'd taken an hour and a half to make supper and eat it.

I left the list in a prominent place for my husband to see when he came home from work at 1:00 a.m. I added the note, "Just in case you wondered what I did all evening."

In the morning I found his tongue-in-cheek response. "Took too long to eat supper." I enjoyed a good laugh.

God can help us simplify and prioritize our lives, if we're tuned in.

∽§

VERSE FOR REFLECTION

I have seen all the things that are done under the sun; all of them are meaningless, a chasing after the wind.
Ecclesiastes 1:14

Naming Our Traditions

A RE YOU LIKE ME in that you always think *other* families are so original and creative in coming up with traditions and rituals that are theirs alone?

I mean, when I hear about families who have a tradition of no TV on Saturday morning, and they sit around in bathrobes playing Scrabble and Monopoly and drinking hot chocolate—it makes me feel my family would qualify for Disintegrated Family of the Year Award. When, I wonder, do such families do their cleaning?

I once interviewed a woman who said their family had a special red plate they used for dinner for someone in the family who had brought their grades up, had a birthday, won an election, or got promoted. I thought that was so neat—but I haven't been able to find an appropriate red plate.

My mom always served the same meal for Saturday night supper: hamburgers, celery, chips, and ice cream.

We rarely went out or had company that night. It was always hamburgers. Once in a great while maybe sloppy joes if we had eaten hamburgers in the middle of the week. That may sound boring, but the memory still stirs wonderful, family-togetherness feelings.

I used to lament that it doesn't often work out for my family to have Saturday night hamburgers. We often go to town or have company that night. In their video series, At Home with the Family, marriage counselors John and Naomi Lederach say that family traditions help to create a healthy family. They give us an identity separate from other families. They help us feel good about our family.

So we don't have to wait till we find some special color of plate or till our kids outgrow Saturday morning cartoons to have our own family traditions. I don't have to lament that my life simply isn't as scheduled as my mom's, so that Saturday night hamburgers rarely work out. There are things we're already doing that *can* be traditions if we decide they are.

For instance, I'm not sure when I started it, but one Sunday morning I was out of doughnuts and other sweets. I concocted quickie sweet rolls by using a can of prepared refrigerator biscuits. Spread the biscuits flat with your fingers. On a bread board, pinch the edges of the biscuits together to make a big, flat piece of dough. Then spread melted butter, brown sugar, and cinnamon on the dough. Roll it up and slice it and bake. Top them if you like, with a simple frosting.

Well, Sunday morning is hardly Sunday morning at our house without those little cinnamon rolls. If I try to skip a Sunday, everyone is put on edge. I had begun to think of them as a nuisance when the Lederachs made me think of them as a tradition we already have. "Talk about your rituals and recognize them for what they are," the Lederachs say.

Now you don't have to start baking Sunday morning cinnamon rolls. But is there something you're already doing that your family looks forward to regularly? I started thinking of other family traditions. Probably my personal favorite is the Sunday evening rule: I don't cook—except for a batch of popcorn. The kids are allowed to eat anything they want, more or less. Frequently they choose cold cereal and milk.

During holiday seasons, lots of family traditions are observed and treasured. For example, do you always drive to the country to choose a Christmas tree at a farm? *Talk* about it with your children as *your* tradition. Name it and it will become special—a memory for family to treasure as years go on.

For years my mother tried to serve oyster soup on Christmas Eve because it was supposed to be a "traditional Christmas Eve supper." But a couple of us kids would only eat the little round oyster crackers and the broth. Then she turned to hot dogs grilled in the fireplace for Christmas Eve, which went over much better! Decide which traditions work in your family, and don't be afraid to discard those which don't. Make traditions part of the glue that builds a healthy family.

Family faith traditions are also important. Making an advent wreath or going to church on Christmas Eve helps draw us closer in faith.

❧

VERSE FOR REFLECTION

Impress them [God's commandments] on your children.
Talk about them when you sit at home and when
you walk along the road, when you lie down
and when you get up.
Deuteronomy 6:7

Music, the Best Medicine

A TENOR WAS BELTING OUT an opera solo on Mr. Roger's Neighborhood. I told my husband, "I think I have a secret yen to be an opera singer. Then people would clap for me instead of telling me to be quiet."

He laughed; while I wasn't really serious, there's something about letting go with a forceful hymn or favorite song in the shower or alone in the car that speaks to my innermost parts. "Music is the language of the soul," as someone has said.

One summer I was having a stressful week. There were meetings at work every day, plus garden work and children at home. I was feeling hurried, harried, behind, uptight. One day, as I was driving home, I was not even thinking about singing. I was thinking of all the work that awaited me on both ends of my commute. Suddenly I realized I was singing a song without consciously deciding to. The words came to me from my past like a gift.

When peace like a river, attendeth my way,
When sorrows like seabillows roll,
Whatever my lot, thou hast taught me to say,
It is well, it is well with my soul.
(Philip Paul Bliss, public domain)

Well, sorrows were not rolling like seabillows in my life at that moment, but the work sure was. Maybe you'll think I'm wacky, but the song seemed at the moment clearly a gift of God, a balm that soothed my frazzled nerves as well as a hot shower and rubdown could have.

I was in tears by the time I got home, not from worry but from joy. I realized how very much God cares and watches over us, like the sparrows.

Remember that great old spiritual, sung so inimitably by Ethel Waters—"His eye is on the sparrow, and I know he watches me," with her voice dipping way down on the "and I"?

This reminiscing about songs reminds me of former hostage Ben Weir's testimony about the time he spent in captivity in Lebanon. In his book *Hostage Bound, Hostage Free* (Westminster, 1987), he says that as day extended into day of unending boredom, the hymns and songs and Bible verses he learned over the years came to him with new force and meaning. "The hymns came tumbling out one after the other," Weir wrote. Some were the great historical hymns of the church, some were gospel or children's tunes.

A neighbor man once commented that he always enjoyed hearing my mother singing or whistling as he drove on the lane past our house. "You always sound so cheerful," he told Mom once.

Mom let out her trademark laugh. "What you don't know is I sometimes sing to forget my troubles!"

Maybe this will start you singing some favorite songs

of your own. Don't worry about what you sound like; find a place alone and pour out your song. I've heard it said that the very act of bringing extra air into your lungs and circulatory system is part of the reason singing makes you feel better. Whatever the reason, we can meet God through the medicine of music.

VERSES FOR REFLECTION

Let the heavens rejoice, let the earth be glad; let the sea resound, and all this is in it; let the fields be jubilant, and everything in them. Then all the trees of the forest will sing for joy.
Psalm 96:11-12

Runaround

T HE RUNAROUND HAPPENS to all of us. We call company XYZ and we get tossed, like a hot potato from department to department. Finally we're so frustrated we resolve never to do business there again.

But one day when it happened to me I just laughed. Not that I'm always so even-tempered. When the fifth person to handle my call asked whom I was trying to reach, it had become so ridiculous I just chuckled and thought about going for a record. I repeated my request. In an instant I was talking to the man I wanted. (A soft answer turneth away wrath, doesn't Proverbs say?)

Several of the people who handle the calls in our own organization discussed this one day at coffee break. "I hate to get calls on line X because I never know whom to give the call to!" said one.

That helped me understand why I sometimes receive the runaround elsewhere. The inner workings of a company are often so complex and political that giving the wrong call to the wrong person can result in confusion and even reprimand.

It's also helpful if we can be as specific as possible in explaining what we want. For instance, call one division of the office I work for and say, "I want to know about your books." Well, the receptionist needs to know whether you just want to place an order or whether you really want information on the philosophy of the organization. That can certainly make a difference in who should receive the call.

So it's helpful to be as patient as possible when connected to Muzak and tossed around like an unwelcome relative.

Now you expect me to say I'm glad it's not like that when I call heaven to connect with the Supreme Operator. We never get put on hold. God's line is never busy.

But maybe that's the problem with prayer. Sometimes we feel like we're getting the royal runaround from God, too. Why aren't our prayers answered? Why do we seem to feel we've received an answer, but a week later the door closes?

A girl was praying about what school to attend. "I've been praying about this for six months. Why don't I get an answer?" she asked her mother in frustration.

Maybe it's because we don't really know what we're praying for. We haven't defined our request, and so we're not ready for an answer. We think we want to talk to the ordering department—when really we should back up and discuss life philosophy with the Almighty.

Or maybe it's because we're inclined to give God the runaround. We tell God, "Thy will be done." Then in the next breath we whisper, "Anything but *that*, dear Lord."

There are many helpful books on learning to pray so we truly communicate with God, and God with us. Maxie Dunnam offers a particularly helpful set of workbooks, *The Workbook of Living Prayer* and *The Workbook of Intercessory Prayer*. Dunnam gives six weeks of daily exercises to discuss in a small group and practice at home. He begins by admitting that often we truly don't know what to ask for, but we can pray for guidance for that. As he says, "When all else fails, follow directions"—referring to the Lord's Prayer, the sample prayer Jesus taught his disciples. We have prayed that prayer so often in public worship settings that we tend not to really mean the words.

One exercise Dunnam suggests I'll leave with you, as a practical way of experiencing closeness with God today. Take the Lord's Prayer (Matt. 6:9-13) and paraphrase it in words that have meaning for you. Perhaps that can be one step toward eliminating the royal runaround and stimulate further study.

❧

Hear my prayer, O Lord; let my cry for help come to you. Do not hide your face from me when I am in distress. Turn your ear to me; when I call, answer me quickly.
Psalm 102:1-2

Money Talks

T HE MINISTER MEANT WELL that Sunday morning when he passed out a crisp new dollar bill to every person in the worship service. It was stewardship season, and perhaps the incident could be dismissed as yet another church ploy to part me and my money.

But that greenback peeking out from my wallet made me uncomfortable for a good while after I got it.

You see, it came with instructions. The note said, "Use it on an investment that will last. Use it to enrich someone's life."

The sermon that morning was based on the story of a wealthy man who gave $5000, $2000, and $1000 to three servants. You know the story. The man who received the $5000 immediately invested it. So did the holder of the $2000. But the third man decided to bury his $1000 in the ground rather than risk losing it on an investment.

Of course, on their master's return the foolish servant was kicked out of the household. We read that a lot of "weeping and gnashing of teeth" went on.

So our minister wasn't just being cute. He wasn't trying to pad the offering plate or to wake up the dozers. He wanted to remind us that all the money we have is a gift from God, pure and simple. And that we are to use *all* our money wisely, investing it in the things that "moth and rust will not corrupt" nor "thieves steal."

But I didn't know what to do with my dollar! It wasn't enough to invest in anything big, which I wouldn't have known how to do even if I did have big money.

I knew the minister wouldn't want me to play the lottery with it because he'd already spoken out against that.

It was hardly worth sending to any charitable organization because once I converted it to a check, supplied envelope and postage, and the computer printed out a receipt, surely more than $1 of "ministry" would be used up.

That dollar was just a nuisance.

At first I left the money on my kitchen table, thinking I wouldn't be tempted to spend it if it wasn't in my wallet. That was *really* a nuisance, with cornflakes and orange juice mucking it up. So I started carrying it around.

When I saw an elderly gentleman standing in front of a housing unit for lower-income older adults, I considered tossing it out my car window for him. Wouldn't that be fun, I thought, to see his reaction? But I decided he'd probably think I was setting a trap for him. Or be offended that I'd consider him a charity case.

Then I had an appointment with a friend to pass on some clothes my six-year-old daughter no longer wore. The woman called to ask to meet me at a different place than previously arranged because she didn't know if she would have enough gas to get there. Here was a place for my dollar bill! A gallon might buy her fifteen miles.

But what if she then expected me to give her money every time I saw her? I didn't really know her that well. Was she just pulling my leg about needing gas?

Charity, it turns out, can be difficult! There is the problem of putting myself on a pedestal as I give, the possibility of welfare dependency, and my concern about my dollars really going where I want them to go. There is a problem of wanting a tax-deductible receipt and wanting to attach strings about how my gift will be used.

That dollar bill certainly spoke to me longer than most sermons. It prodded me from my wallet, getting older and more frayed and dirtier with each passing day.

"Silly, lazy woman," I suddenly imagined the Master saying. "Why don't you at least put my money on deposit with the bankers, so that it will earn interest?"

Weep, weep. Gnash, gnash.

Do you think the credit union would snicker if I made a $1 deposit?

✍

VERSE FOR REFLECTION

For if the willingness is there, the gift is acceptable according to what one has, not according to what he does not have.
2 Corinthians 8:12

Second Grade Forgiveness

I T HAPPENED IN SECOND GRADE. I can still see Sandy bending by the shelves that stored our gym shoes at school, desperately trying to scrub mud off my pretty red sneakers with wet paper towels.

"It won't come off," she said, shaking her head and close to tears. She had borrowed them without asking and worn them at recess, out in the mud. "I'm sorry," she said over and over. It was certainly a forgivable offense, but it seemed a large sin to second graders.

"Let's all hate Sandy," my friend Sharon conspired on my behalf. So we passed hate notes until Sandy was properly ostracized and punished.

Again I'm reminded that childhood can be a terribly lonely, cruel time. I'm still ashamed, even though we soon forgot about the muddy shoes and Sandy was our friend once again.

Sometimes we look at people who've forgiven deep

hurts—a spouse forgiving an adulterous mate, a child forgiving an abusive parent—and think it's wonderful they could find it in their hearts to forgive.

In Matthew 18:23-35, we read the parable of the unmerciful servant who has a huge debt wiped clean, then refuses to go easy on a man who owes *him* a few dollars.

When the king throws the unmerciful servant into prison we read that this is how God will treat us unless we forgive others.

This makes me realize again that forgiveness is not just something nice to do out of the bigness of our hearts. It's not an extra, not just polite manners. It's *required* of anyone who calls herself Christian. We have been forgiven much. So we must also forgive.

That doesn't mean it's easy. Like second graders, we have a hard time coughing up the words and meaning them. We have a hard time asking, giving, and receiving forgiveness. Why is it so hard?

Granting forgiveness is something God does, and does well! When we extend forgiveness, we're behaving a little like God. So no wonder it's hard to do. And then we're supposed to forgive again and again—as many times as "seventy times seven" is the figurative way the Bible puts it.

I don't think this rules out making changes in your life so that whoever is hurting or sinning against you can't do it again. If a spouse persists in adulterous affairs or promiscuity, making a mockery of your wedding vows; if your life or the lives of your children are threatened by abuse; if your mental stability is at stake; if a "friend" seems to enjoy cutting you down in public—then perhaps the loving thing is to remove yourself from the situation so that the hurting and need for forgiveness does not go on in an endless cycle.

It is often this refusal to cooperate with a cycle of

abuse or hurt that helps shock the offending person into making a change. Forgiveness can become too cheap—a "second grade" forgiveness.

If there is someone you need to forgive, may you find it in your heart to take that step. If you need to ask for forgiveness, may you be encouraged to take that step also. And if you've exhausted all avenues of help and offered repeated forgiveness, may you find the courage to take the necessary steps to change your situation. We see God more clearly when our slates with God and other human beings are clean.

᪥

VERSE FOR REFLECTION

Do not judge, and you will not be judged. Do not condemn,
and you will not be condemned. Forgive,
and you will be forgiven.
Luke 6:37

Barriers on Barrier Island

ONE SUMMER MY FAMILY vacationed on a barrier island off the Atlantic coast. (A barrier island, if you've forgotten your geography, runs parallel to a larger body of land and protects the land from the pounding surf.)

The island lived up to my dreams, with its pristine clapboard houses and salty old sea mariners. But it had some "barriers" I had not counted on.

We were traveling with my parents, and my father was disabled at the time and needed to use a wheelchair most of the time. We had found a motel with access for wheelchairs. But the ramp was so steep there was no way he could wheel his chair himself as he preferred. The bathroom door in the motel room was much too small for any wheelchair. The motel's only telephone was on a patio three steps up. It was a fine motel. But it was not accessible for the truly wheelchair-bound.

No big deal. Dad took the inconveniences in his usual

good-natured manner. We were happy for a ramp that allowed him to wheel as far as the top of the beach (although not down on the beach).

But the barrier that disappointed me most was such a little thing I'm almost embarrassed to mention it. The first evening on the island we had spied an old-fashioned ice cream parlor, complete with a screened front porch that had tables, antique wire-backed parlor stools, and mauve-striped canopies on the windows. We made a mental date with that ice cream shop, promising to treat ourselves on our last evening.

At the appointed time, we strolled and rolled to the shop, only to notice for the first time that there were about five steps leading up to the porch. Not much, but we decided rather than maneuver Dad's wheelchair up those steps we'd just eat on a bench in the yard. Once again I saw how such little things can impede the normal pursuit of pleasure for a person in a wheelchair.

I realize a ramp for such a small shop may have been too costly. Certainly huge strides have been made in recent years for wheelchair accessibility. But more, in this case, is never enough. Along with scientific advancements in medicine comes the fact that more and more of us may face part of life handicapped instead of dead. I know my father was more pleased to be enjoying ice cream with three of his granddaughters than put out that we couldn't eat on the romantic little porch.

But there was a second barrier on that island. Again, I can't really blame the proprietors, but it was a disappointment nevertheless. We had noticed a restaurant bearing my father's boyhood nickname. Naturally we thought it would be fun to eat there. The entrance was flat; no problem with wheelchairs. But when we got to the entrance it said, "Please no children under twelve." Another restaurant wouldn't allow anyone under sixteen!

Again, I can understand barring children under six. I don't enjoy eating in fancy restaurants myself when I'm worrying about spills, screams, and dirty diapers. But I know plenty of kids aged six to fifteen who could manage white glove manners for one hour. I understand the owner's logic but it still hurts to be excluded.

Our society, many have pointed out, is not really as pro-children as it professes. Perhaps we should take the Club Med way out, which provides all-day child care and activities. Keep the kids in kennels, out of the way.

Then I recall with pleasure all the trips I enjoyed with my parents when we were small. Niagara Falls will never thrill me as an adult the way it did when I was a child.

Sometimes children are barred from worship services, too. When our children were small I enjoyed having the children in the nursery during worship, but I also enjoyed letting them participate in worship at times. They could hum along with the songs and move in rhythm to the music. I guess the lesson I've learned from my barrier island is to work to make sure that at least our churches are places where both children and those in wheelchairs are welcomed—both by the nature of the buildings and the nature of the people.

❧

VERSE FOR REFLECTION
*I rejoiced with those who said to me, "Let us go
to the house of the Lord."*
Psalm 122:1

Make Room For
a Child

I REMEMBER ONE MORNING when Doreen was just approaching three years of age. She woke up too early, so I put her at the kitchen table to eat while I continued the all-important business of getting ready for work.

"Sit there and watch me," Doreen requested with milk dribbling on her chin as I rushed through the kitchen.

Again I was stopped in my tracks by a child, causing me to consider what is really important in life. Is it more crucial to wash the dishes before going to work, or to spend a few quiet moments with my child?

I'm convinced children are placed in our lives to remind us of priorities. They tug at our trousers. They pout "Pity me!" And sometimes just when you were beginning to enjoy the empty nest, they move back home. Children remind us, if we'll listen, that we were children once too who needed attention, hugs, and direction.

I remember reading about parents from less developed countries who put their young children alone on planes and sent them to better-off countries in search of a better future (*Newsweek*, August 28, 1988). The parents had heard that countries like West Germany (at that time) didn't require a visa for children under sixteen and immediately provided for children through excellent social services.

The children were sent from Sri Lanka, Afghanistan, Lebanon, Turkey and other places where poverty or war threatened their well-being. Of course there were racketeers involved too, charging parents three times the price of a normal airplane ticket to get their children out with no questions asked.

These were real E.T.s, little kids dropped into a new world like aliens from outer space, homesick and heartsick from their loss, believing their parents would join them as soon as they had the money (a futile hope). The story made me weep. One *more* story of children in heartrending circumstances.

Who will make room for a child? As we rush around with busy schedules, will we make room as we rush around? Consider the child Jesus, ushered unceremoniously into the world while people scurried about paying taxes and finding hotel rooms?

Jesus was orphaned, in a sense, by God; but he was taken under the wings of Mary and Joseph. Mary and Joseph did for him all the things normal parents do. They wiped his nose, cleaned messes, fixed food, kissed hurts, mended toys, told stories, patched squabbles with siblings. This was divine work for Mary and Joseph.

But parenting can be divine work for us too, nurturing sons and daughters of God into beautiful men and women.

Just because Mary and Joseph were raising a divine

child didn't make it easy. Remember when Jesus was twelve and "got lost" from his parents? His parents expressed outright exasperation when they found him. And surely there were many other incidents we'll never know about.

I may still blow my fuse when Doreen wants milk poured on her cereal, Tanya needs help picking out an outfit, and Michelle's trying to find her library book. But thinking of parenting as divine work makes my fuse a little longer. Thinking of parents who are so desperate for a future for their children that they send them to a new country makes me want to hold and cherish my child with milk dribbled on her chin—and even helps me see past the dirty dishes in the sink.

How do I make room for the children around me?

∾§

VERSE FOR REFLECTION

When Jesus saw this, he was indignant. He said to them, "Let the little children come to me, and do not hinder them, for the kingdom of God belongs to such as these."
Mark 10:14

Scenes from a Life

I T LOOKS LIKE YOU HAVE tinsel in your hair," my oldest daughter said one day. And so it did: a shiny, glittering strand of gray highlighted the top of my crown.

Don't get me wrong. I'm not rejoicing about getting a few gray hairs. But seen through her eyes the hair was as sparkling as a piece of Christmas froth—a "silver thread," as in the old song.

"Mommy, why do you have those blue lines on your legs," the littlest one often asks.

"Well, they're my veins and they stick out because I'm getting old," I tell her again.

"I don't want you to be old," she replies quietly. Ah, yes, dear. Me neither.

A touching video, *The Estate Sale*, gets at some of these themes. The movie artfully switches back and forth between scenes of two women going through the belongings of a deceased couple and scenes from that couple's life—moving into their first home, a child's birthday party, a New Year's Eve party, and finally a graduation celebration the father canceled out of at the last minute because of business.

Aw, come on, I thought. *What parent would miss a child's graduation except for extreme emergency?* So it isn't too hard to figure out in the video why this couple's children didn't seem to want any family photographs or drawings the architect-father had produced. Indeed, the very idea of the treasured accumulations of a lifetime being pawed through by flippant, uncaring strangers at an estate sale or auction gives most of us something to think about.

I was previewing the video for a meeting when all of a sudden I looked at my watch. Horrors! It was ten minutes to twelve. I had promised the four-year-old she *wouldn't* be the last child picked up at nursery school that day. "Mommy," she had said that morning, "remember, I don't want to be last today."

"Yes, dear," I had said, "I'll try to be early. I can't promise to be first, but I won't be last."

I sped downtown (at the speed limit, though) and luckily found a convenient parking place. It was five minutes till twelve. There was no way all the other children could have been picked up already.

I looked in the door. There stood Doreen toward the back of the room, hood securely tied under her chin, looking very grave. And then it hit me. Perhaps I wouldn't think of canceling out of a child's graduation ceremonies. But to Doreen, my showing up on time was, at this moment in her life, as important.

Her face lit up. No, I hadn't been the first, but at least there were still four other children waiting. Her hand felt better than usual tucked in mine as we walked toward the car. For once I didn't hurry her, and we enjoyed the sights and sounds of a busy downtown.

The video ends with the one woman leaving the sale to go and call her own mother. "I just want you to know that I love you very much," she says, voice catching. "I was wondering if it would be okay if we came down for the weekend."

If I'm never late to pick up the children at school, never miss a recital or a school play—will this guarantee me lots of letters, calls, and visits when I'm really gray? Of course not. If there are unavoidable emergencies and I end up disappointing my children greatly, will this mean I'll have ungrateful, ill-mannered children? I hope not. Parents make choices they sometimes regret; adult children do too.

But I think there are patterns to our lives that increase the odds of our children growing up to be a blessing to us in our old age. Do I worry more about *things*—about my next acquisition—than the happiness of human beings? Do I take time for them when it counts, not just when it's convenient? If I've made choices in the past that I now regret, can I reach out to someone even now?

⋖⋗

VERSE FOR REFLECTION

For I will pour water on the thirsty land, and streams on the dry ground; I will pour out my Spirit on your offspring, and my blessing on your descendants.
Isaiah 44:3

Life in the
Truck Lane

A NUMBER OF RETIRED PEOPLE volunteer at our office to assemble *by hand* the tens of thousands of colorful calendars we offer every year for distribution by hundreds of churches.

One volunteer was going slowly up the stairs. He paused with his hand on the rail to let me pass and quipped, "You'll have to excuse me, I'm in the truck lane these days." Little did he know he was God's special messenger to me that day, making me think about life and how I was living it.

His smile seemed to say he was enjoying life in the truck lane, but I know that is not the case with all retirees.

"I feel I'm able finally to devote my time to the things I want to be doing," said Myra (all names changed) in talking about her retirement. "I have never felt so useful in the church and for God as in this stage of my life."

"Oh, I feel exactly the opposite of that," said Nancy,

her voice on the edge of breaking as she shared from her pain. "I feel so useless. The ironic part is that I used to work with senior citizens, counseling them on 'how to prepare for retirement.' Now I can't listen to my own advice!"

Part of Nancy's frustration stems from health limitations, a factor for many in the truck lane.

Then there are many like Elizabeth, blessed to pursue a career at home all her life never having had to work outside the home. "When do I get to retire?" she says, laughing. People tend to dump on her all the jobs "working" folks don't have time for.

I'm not about to give advice on how to have a happy retirement, since my words, like Nancy's, would likely ring hollow when I get there. But I do wonder—how can we prepare to move into the retirement years and still feel good about ourselves?

Perhaps the answer lies in a look at our culture. If we grew up envying those able to enjoy life from a slower lane, then maybe moving to retired status wouldn't be so difficult for some. Instead of the volunteer apologizing to *me* for slowing down my progress, I should have been apologizing to him for rushing by him, lost in my own busyness.

Surely one of the hardest parts about retirement these days is facing health and physical limitations. Although articles about retirement seem to highlight folks who are running marathons and heading big corporations at seventy-five, that just makes it more painful for those who can't do the things they'd like. A simple thing like not being able to drive at night curtails many involvements.

Again there are no easy answers, except the testimony of those who say getting involved in the lives of others as they are able helps keep the mind off the pain. One thing

Nancy has found to occupy her time is writing delightful stories from her childhood to share with her grandchildren and a regular writer's group.

I suppose part of the human condition is always envying others. As I rush to work, part of me wishes very much to be in the truck lane of retirement. Another part of me knows that when I'm seventy-five, I'll look wistfully at people hurrying to work or harried mothers shopping with their small children and wish I could go back in time. Perhaps what is needed is balance—the ability to move back and forth between lanes to enjoy true leisure even in the hurried years; and relationships and tasks to keep you moving in the slower years.

Whatever lane we're in—truck, middle, or fast, what we need is the ability to accept it with the serenity of my elderly friend on the stairway. And the courage to *change* lanes now and then if we need to.

ಈ§

VERSES FOR REFLECTION

The fear of the Lord is the beginning of wisdom, and knowledge of the Holy One is understanding. For through me your days will be many, and years will be added to your life.
Proverbs 9:10-11

Look Like You Know What You're Doing

AN INTERIM PASTOR at our church told a wonderful story of a time when he was in Chicago for a meeting and the late Hubert Humphrey was scheduled for a campaign speech at the same hotel. This pastor suddenly became aware that the presidential hopeful would soon enter through a nearby door. Around him was a great deal of official hubbub with lots of Secret Service men and people with clearance badges.

This pastor decided he would stick around until someone asked him to leave. He had on a detective-style trench coat. One guard nodded to him; the pastor nodded back. He just kept up an air of "I know what I'm doing here" and soon Humphrey passed within arm's length.

"Look like you know what you're doing," is good advice—at least as valuable as all the other rules your folks sent with you to kindergarten. I seem to recall saying the same thing as a teenager when my friends and I would try a crazy stunt at school or the mall. In fact, I'm told that the official creed of a certified mechanic is, "I don't know what I'm doing but I sure am an expert at it."

The difference between kids and adults is that kids (at least to a certain age) think adults know what they're doing. Doctors are nothing less than magicians, dispensing cures in bottles of bubble-gum-flavored medicine. Clerks in an ordinary store are thought to own *all those toys,* which they give you in exchange for some drab pieces of paper. Mom can always go to the bank to get more of those pieces of paper, and Dad (after repairing a broken toy) can fix *anything!*

The older I get the more I realize that all the people I once thought knew what they were doing are often guessing, hunching, even bumbling along. Now that I go to doctors younger than I am, I can see their insecurities —the times they haven't got a clue and rule out the possibilities like ruling out answers on a multiple choice test. Not that I don't trust them—they still know more than I do about medical things. But I finally realize that they're human, too.

Knowing that some people are guessing as they go should make us realize we have to take responsibility to ask enough questions to find out if the advice is reliable. When in doubt, we can get a second opinion, do our own research, talk to people who have been through it.

Perhaps our society's tendency to sue over things so trivial as a broken thumbnail is one result of people acting like they know what they are doing when they don't, or people putting unlimited faith in those who act like they know what they are doing.

Somehow it is comforting for me to hear a doctor

sorting through available treatment options. This demystifies the medical world and makes me feel more responsible for my care—and perhaps less likely to sue. It helps me feel more human when I find myself in a situation where I haven't got a clue but need to proceed anyway.

All of this is true only to a certain extent. When I go under a surgeon's knife, I don't want someone who is guessing as they go. All of us become experts at the things we do everyday. The school secretary is an expert at sniffing out the fake excuses from the real things. The farmer knows when the corn is ready to pick from the sight, smell, and feel of the ear. It's fun to reach the point in life where, no matter what your field, you feel like you really do have some expertise to offer. It's one reward of growing older—you don't have to bluff.

Though it's not always possible to know God's way on a given issue, it's comforting to know that God *does* know. We humans are bound by all sorts of limitations. God alone is limitless, all-knowing, all-loving. I can rest (usually) in the comfort of that knowledge.

ಆ

VERSE FOR REFLECTION

Who is wise and understanding among you? Let him show it by his good life, by deeds done in the humility that comes from wisdom.
James 3:13

Just Call Me Scientifically Fuzzy

Y OU MAY REMEMBER THE REPORT from the U.S. National Science Foundation several years back saying that millions of adults appear to be scientifically illiterate about such things as whether the earth goes around the sun or vice versa, and what the three components of an atom are.

Yes, I studied all of that stuff one time. And I admit I should know these things as quickly as I know my driver's license number. But when it came right down to some of the questions on the list, I panicked. I couldn't answer with certainty.

Yet I rebel at the thought of being labeled scientifically illiterate. Scientifically *fuzzy* maybe, but not illiterate. Or maybe I'm just scientifically apathetic. I always figured the best thing I learned in school was how to look things up.

I was always better at broad concepts than specific

facts; I loved essay exams, hated true-and-false tests. I decided the main thing I needed to know about the universe was that somehow it all worked. About science: remember that everything is orderly; about math: remember everything is logical. In short, the whole field of math and science is everything I'm not—logical and orderly.

Since that long-ago day when I learned the precise rotation of planets and things, I've been busying my brain with other things. Let's see. I learned my wedding vows, and my spouse's important identification numbers. I've learned the names and faces of thousands of new people (as well as dozens of cats and dogs), the names and authors of hundreds of books, the word-processing intricacies of several computer programs.

I've written seven books; remembered six Lamaze breathing techniques; kept in mind the due dates, birth dates, and doctor appointments of all my children. I've learned how to draw blueprints for mobile homes, wait on tables, and cook short orders. I've learned to avoid nitrates, eat bran, and count fat grams. And, of course, you understand I'm not bragging, just explaining. No wonder my brain is scientifically fuzzy!

Okay, so I never was a whiz at science. And the researchers have a point—it's a shame we know (or remember) as little as we do about basic scientific stuff. It embarrasses me to admit my fuzziness. But I figure it's time all we scientifically fuzzy types come out of the closet. Maybe we can band together, declare ourselves a new minority, and they'll set up a whole foundation to tutor us in Basic Scientific Education just in case the question of what orbits what comes up at my next dinner party.

I care, I really do care. I understand why, in a world where the future of the planet depends on scientifically aware citizens, people worry about those of us who've forgotten some basic facts. It's disturbing that on the most prosperous continent of the earth many are information-poor. Indeed, we could be put to shame by eight-year-olds from much poorer countries. I just confess a bit of information overload.

Biblical illiteracy is another problem. I'm amazed at how many people seem to be fuzzy on some basic Bible stories and passages. And these are people who've grown up in the church! One philosophy about teaching Bible stories to young children seems to say, "They can't understand the good old stories; teach them basics like love and sharing and they'll pick up the specific stories later."

Another approach is to read the stories along with teaching about love and sharing; the minds of young children can absorb so much (before they reach my stage of information-overload!). The caution is to teach them in a way that doesn't frighten children (you can leave out the goriest parts of David and Goliath, for instance).

While I might complain of brain-overload, the world that God made continues to amaze, interest, and delight me. The world of science can help us marvel at the infinite mind of God. It's also remarkable that God created us with minds that soak up as much as they do. We can live in such a way that our education—though formally over—never stops.

~§

VERSE FOR REFLECTION

"For who had known the mind of the Lord that he may instruct him?" But we have the mind of Christ.
1 Corinthians 2:16

A Plain Trip
Through Life

WHAT STARTED OUT as a plain ordinary trip home at Christmas one year deteriorated rapidly into a B-grade movie. Oldest daughter started throwing up roughly one half hour into the mountain portion of our trip. Youngest daughter followed suit soon after—but at the tender age of twenty-two months, she could rarely be counted on to hit the "sick" bag.

This would have all been par for a normal trip home. But getting stopped for barely speeding was not. Several miles out of a little burg called Russel's Point, an eager young officer pulled my husband over and returned to the squad car to write out a $48 ticket. Suddenly the officer ran back to our window as if we had won the lottery saying, "You're in luck. Merry Christmas. I've been called to an accident."

Husband: "What do you mean, sir?"

Officer: "I mean I won't write you a ticket! Merry Christmas!"

Of course, it wasn't so lucky for whoever had the accident. We were just trying to decide whether to feel good about this or not when Stuart tried to restart the car. Dead. Nothing. No lights, no juice. Nothing. As he rattled around under the hood trying to figure out what was wrong, he was heard to mutter, "We've got to hurry and get out of here or that police officer will come back and *still* write me that ticket."

Fortunately, someone stopped to help, so Stuart left to find a wrecker. Unfortunately, that left me alone trying to cheer up three very worried little ones.

Kids: "What's going to happen? Will we ever get to Grandpa's?"

Mom: "Of course, we'll get there. We may get to ride in a wrecker and sleep in a motel first, though. Just think! This time, instead of having a plain ordinary trip to Grandma's, we'll have an adventure!"

To which oldest daughter replied—with all the smarts she had acquired by the ripe age of six: "I'd rather just have a plain trip."

Unfortunately, the baby had to dirty a diaper while we were waiting for my husband to come back. Fortunately, there was a small flashlight in the car. Unfortunately, it wouldn't work. When I opened it to check the batteries, one slipped down the seat crack. Fortunately, I did get the diaper changed. Unfortunately, I didn't do the greatest job in the dark, and now the youngster really smelled swell, but I'm getting off the subject.

About this time the police officer really did reappear and I was glad my husband had disappeared. What cop would ticket a woman stranded with three kids three days before Christmas? I *was* glad to know that the accident apparently wasn't serious since the cop had come back so fast. I assured him that help was on the way and again he wished us a Merry Christmas.

To make a now boring story short, the battery cables were cleaned, the car started, and the Davises were blessed with a very ordinary trip all the rest of the way to Grandma's house.

Everyone has stories of horrible travel adventures to tell. One of my favorites involves the time we were charged $13 for a gallon of antifreeze. A close second is the time the officer stopped us for stealing watermelons. A family favorite is the time we had to eat orange-pineapple ice cream for breakfast near Niagara Falls. And then there was the time I found myself sliding backward down an icy interstate with a truck staring me in the face.

It's funny how even the most miserable of experiences becomes glorified and is remembered fondly as time washes away the frustrated feelings and leaves us mostly with precious, irreplaceable memories. I'm glad we were made that way—with time healing at least some of the hurt but not robbing us of the best memories.

I'm getting old enough now that I realize hardly anyone gets a "plain" trip. The journeys of all of us are marked by detours, stop signs, accidents, and fines. What deep, sustaining comfort it is to know that God is beside us all along the way—sometimes carrying us, sometimes guiding, sometimes walking hand in hand. God is here.

❧

VERSE FOR REFLECTION
Let us throw off everything that hinders and the sin that so easily entangles, and let us run with perseverance the race marked out for us.
Hebrews 12:1b

The Author

M elodie Miller Davis is a writer/producer for the Media Ministries department of Mennonite Board of Missions, Harrisonburg, Virginia.

Melodie has worked for Media Ministries since her 1975 graduation from Eastern Mennonite College (Harrisonburg) with degrees in English and Spanish. As part of her work she writes a newspaper column, "Another Way," which appears in about eighteen papers. She also oversees production of print media materials for Mennonite congregations and the larger denomination.

Melodie is a member of the National Federation of Press Women as well as the Council on Church and Media. She is a local editor of *Living* an experimental "Good News" tabloid in two communities. She is the author of seven books. Her most recent, which tells about a year in Barcelona, Spain, is *Departure* (Herald Press, 1991).

She and her husband, Stuart, are parents of Michelle (1981), Tanya (1983), and Doreen (1986), the inspiration for many of these meditations. The Davises belong to

Trinity Presbyterian Church in Harrisonburg, a house-church based congregation which they have both served as elders.

Melodie grew up on a farm near Goshen, Indiana, where she learned to find God while cultivating long rows of corn, gathering hundreds of eggs, and shelling bushels of peas. During her year in Barcelona, she also learned to find God down smelly subway stairs and on crowded sidewalks.